BUYING ANTIQUES

General Guide

A. W. COYSH joined the BBC in the 1940s and for nearly twenty-five years was connected with the programme output of the West Region, particularly in the field of Talks and Topicality. He was responsible for launching BBC's *Talking About Antiques*, the radio offshoot of *Going for a Song*. His interest in antiques ranges over a wide field and he is especially keen on English pottery. He has also written *Blue and White Transfer Ware, 1780–1840* and produced an *Antique Buyer's Dictionary of Names*.

JOHN KING came to Bristol in 1964 to work as a free-lance radio journalist. He became research assistant on BBC-TV's *Going for a Song* in 1965 and subsequently producer. In 1969 he had two network television programmes running at the same time, and in October of that year he was awarded the Fleming Memorial Trophy by the Bristol and South Western Centre of the Royal Television Society. In 1970 he produced a new series of programmes *Collector's World* for BBC-2 which commenced in August.

The David & Charles Series

BUYING ANTIQUES
General Guide

A. W. COYSH
and
J. KING

UNABRIDGED

PAN BOOKS LTD : LONDON

First published in this form 1968 by
David & Charles (Publishers) Ltd.
This edition published 1971 by Pan Books Ltd,
33 Tothill Street, London, S.W.1

ISBN 0 330 02676 3

Printed in Great Britain by
Cox & Wyman Ltd., London, Reading and Fakenham

CONTENTS

ILLUSTRATIONS IN PHOTOGRAVURE

(between pages 84 and 85)

LINE DRAWINGS

ACKNOWLEDGEMENTS

We are greatly indebted to Arthur Negus, Bernard Price, and Paul and Ken Smith who read the manuscript of this book and offered many helpful suggestions; also to John Bone for the drawings, to Michael Wagen who took the photographs, and to the BBC for permission to use them.

A. W. COYSH
J. KING

FOREWORD BY ARTHUR NEGUS

Most books on antiques assume that the reader has some knowledge of the subject. This book makes no such assumption. It has been written for the interested amateur and for this reason should prove useful in helping him to identify works of art and in directing his attention to some of the main points to be considered when buying antiques in saleroom or shop.

Arthur G. Negus

CHAPTER ONE

BUYING ANTIQUES

WHAT is an antique? To all intents and purposes, any useful or decorative object produced by artists or craftsmen is regarded by the trade as an antique provided it is more than 100 years old. This is the period generally recognized by antique dealers though most organizers of antique fairs will only accept furniture made before 1830. The object must be sufficiently esteemed and sought after to have value, and it may be coveted for various reasons – its beauty, craftsmanship, rarity or curiosity.

It is not wise to assume that all the goods for sale in shops which bear the sign 'Antiques' must be over 100 years old. Many shops and dealers sell items made during the last 100 years if they have a special interest for the antique-buying public – reproduction, *art nouveau* and late Victorian articles eighty or ninety years old which will become antique relatively soon and for this reason are attractive to people who are buying as a form of investment.

It is possible, even in a relatively short period, to develop a 'sense' about antiques: mistakes will certainly be made but confidence will soon grow, particularly if a special study is made of one field. If, for example, it is decided to concentrate on porcelain, or even porcelain of one period or of one maker, then knowledge and experience will accumulate relatively quickly, and you will soon feel able to back your own judgement and to buy with confidence.

What are the main fields? Among the most popular is

silver, though much of this is expensive and beyond the price the average person can afford. Sheffield plate, however, can still be obtained quite reasonably. So can some furniture, especially that of the early and mid-Victorian periods and, surprisingly enough, some quite old pieces of oak and country-made furniture. Glass is a difficult subject. There is so little to be seen in a piece of glass which helps the collector to date it – and it can easily be copied. Nor is it easy for the beginner to recognize faked glassware.

Pottery is of wide interest and remains one of the most rewarding fields for the collector. It has always been cheaper than porcelain because it was made in large quantities for those who could not afford the finer wares. In fact, poorer folk often demanded earthenware designs similar to the porcelain ones used by the wealthy. They also created a form of cottage art that delightfully reflects many of the sports, manners and customs of the time.

As a result of this demand, fine craftsmen appeared in the potteries: men like Ralph and Enoch Wood. Much of their work, particularly their figures, attracted a good deal of attention and was bought by people well up in the social scale. Later, there was also a considerable middle-class market for pottery, and manufacturers such as Spode turned out beautiful dinner-sets in simply decorated transfer ware.

Prints and paintings provide another profitable hunting-ground. Armed with a few essential facts and a discriminating personal taste, even the amateur can build up a small collection which will increase in value and provide constant pleasure.

Some people have no urge to 'collect' but enjoy having beautiful things around them in their homes – good antique furniture, a few fine pieces of decorative glass or porcelain, the odd print or painting. Fair enough. They will enhance the look of any room and bring themselves and their friends much real enjoyment.

But let us begin at the beginning. What is the best way to set about buying antiques? If you know absolutely nothing, the obvious thing to do is to go to a reputable antique dealer, tell him what you want and ask him to help you. Very often he will be willing to give you a written guarantee that the article you buy is a genuine piece of a certain period, style and date. You will obviously have to pay more than you might have to for a similar article in a saleroom because you are paying for his judgement and experience and he also has to make a fair profit. But until you feel you can rely on your own judgement this may well be the wisest thing to do. On the other hand, you will obviously be a little less likely to pick up a real bargain in this way than by hunting around second-hand stores and junk shops.

Then there are the public auctions, sometimes held in a saleroom, sometimes in a private house when the executors of an estate decide to dispose of the contents. It is possible to learn a great deal from these sales, particularly about current values, even without actually buying. But if the intention is to buy, it is wise to avoid being carried away by the excitement. Decide in advance the maximum price you are prepared to pay *before the bidding starts*. Resist any temptation to go higher or you may well regret it afterwards. On the other hand, never be afraid of bidding firmly and making your presence felt.

Auctioneers can no longer put the onus on the buyer to decide whether their description of an object is accurate or not. The Misrepresentation Act now provides a clear remedy for anyone who has been misled by a false catalogue description. The buyer has the right to revoke a contract within a reasonable period irrespective of whether the description was made in good faith or not.

Nevertheless, check everything very thoroughly and do remember that some repairs are invisible to the naked eye. If you intend to buy a particularly expensive item it is always advisable to have it thoroughly checked in advance by an expert. For example, a skilfully repaired piece of porcelain must be examined under ultra-violet radiation to reveal the hidden damage. Well-executed repairs to furniture are often done with old wood and can only be detected by the most experienced eye. Most auctioneers will respect your caution and will readily agree to a detailed inspection, but it must normally be carried out during the time when the objects are on view to the public. Inspection of this kind would rarely be allowed during the actual sale. So it is wise to view as early as possible in case you need to consult an expert or look up the reference books.

Attending auction sales is a time-consuming business: it may be necessary to wait several hours before the particular item you are interested in comes 'under the hammer'. It is worth remembering that most auctioneers average from sixty to 100 lots an hour. Check with the firm responsible: they know their auctioneers. If you want to leave the saleroom for a time, it is possible to work out from the catalogue roughly when the item which interests you will be sold. If you find it impossible to attend a sale but can manage to view the lots at some other time to decide what you want to buy, ask one of the saleroom staff to bid for you, telling him the price you are prepared to pay for any given lot. It is usual to give him a gratuity for this service: about one shilling in the pound would be reasonable on most purchases, though obviously it should be a little more on a very cheap item. Finally, it is a mistake to be in a hurry to buy. Buying is an art in itself. Have a good look round, and compare the quality, condition and price of what the shops have to offer before making a final decision. A real lover of antiques never gives up the search; he keeps looking for what he wants. The very article may come in to an antique shop from a private house or a saleroom at any hour of any day and, if it is a 'good buy', it will soon have gone again.

A good motto for the inexperienced is 'if in doubt, leave it alone'. To recognize a real bargain needs knowledge and experience, but the possibility that a real 'discovery' may one day be made always adds interest and excitement to the search.

CHAPTER TWO

FURNITURE

ONE of the greatest pleasures for those who are developing an interest in antiques comes from the detective work involved in 'placing' an article. When was it made? Where was it made? Who made it?

How does an auctioneer decide on the descriptions he will issue in his sale catalogue? The 'Sheraton mahogany bow-fronted sideboard' and the 'William IV oval cake-dish, pierced and chased, by Charles Fox, London 1835, 22½ oz', for example. Many salerooms employ experts who advise on such things. We aim to help the amateur to identify items and to understand some of the descriptions he will inevitably meet in the antique shop or the auction room.

The first problem is to decide roughly when an article was made; in other words, the period to which it belongs. The period timetable for antiques in Britain on the opposite page is closely related to the reigning British Sovereigns. It covers the seventeenth, eighteenth and nineteenth centuries and refers particularly to furniture. In earlier Tudor times, furnishings were sparse and very utilitarian in design, consisting almost entirely of trestle tables, stools, beds and chests made of oak: carving was very simple. Items of this kind are rare.

In Stuart times, however, the demand for furniture increased and craftsmen began to develop wood-turning as a means of embellishment; carving began to lose favour. Screws had not been invented at this time so parts were secured by mortice and tenon joints held together by wooden pins or dowels. This was joinery as distinct from

Period Timetable for Antiques in Britain	Reigning Sovereign	French Influences on British Styles
ELIZABETHAN 1600	ELIZABETH.	
JACOBEAN (Conventionally used for antiques of the reigns of James I and Charles I)	JAMES I 1603-25	
	CHARLES I 1625-49	
CROMWELLIAN or COMMONWEALTH, 1649-59	CHARLES II 1649-85	LOUIS XIV 1643-1715 A period distinguished by the pomp which surrounded Versailles. Large ornate furniture, often gilded
RESTORATION		
	JAMES II 1685-8	
WILLIAM and MARY } Period of QUEEN ANNE } Dutch Influence 1700	WILLIAM AND MARY 1689-1702	
	QUEEN ANNE 1702-14	
	GEORGE I 1714-27	LOUIS XV 1715-1774 A more delicate 'rococo' style of decoration and inlay but very intricate. Some influence on Chippendale
THE GEORGIAN PERIOD was noted for its designers, especially for furniture. These men gave their names to styles which are widely recognized (See Fig 3)	GEORGE II 1727-60	
	GEORGE III 1760-1820	LOUIS XVI 1774-93 Simpler and more delicate forms
1800		
The term 'REGENCY' is used for the period from 1800 to 1830	THE REGENCY 1811-20	EMPIRE to about 1830 During the Directoire period, after the French Revolution, a new style developed in imitation of the styles of early Greece and Rome. Empire furniture was strong, massive and decorated with gilt bronze mounts. Greatly influenced British Regency style
	GEORGE IV 1820-30	
	WILLIAM IV 1830-7	
VICTORIAN	VICTORIA 1837-1901	
1900		
	EDWARD VII 1901-10	

Figure 1   THE ANTIQUE PERIODS

cabinet-making. Hinges and lock plates were of iron. The early Stuart furniture of the reigns of James I and Charles I is commonly referred to as Jacobean. Then came the Civil War and the furniture made in Cromwellian or Commonwealth times between 1649 and 1659 became plainer, in keeping with the puritanical philosophy of the day. In the Restoration period which followed in the reign of Charles II, the pendulum swung back. New designs emerged: the spiral twist and woven cane seats and backs appeared in chairs, and 'grandfather' or long-case clocks were made for the first time.

The William and Mary and Queen Anne periods produced what is generally regarded as some of the finest English furniture. By now the craftsmen were taking a great pride in the finish of an article and were paying much more attention to overall balance of design. Veneering and inlay work flourished and carving had almost been forgotten. Furniture in these periods was often small – a highly desirable quality today.

As George I came to the throne, furniture-making was becoming more of an art than a craft and designs became more elegant with no loss of strength. The cabinet-maker was coming into his own. This process developed throughout the Georgian period, reaching its height in the reign of George III.

The term 'Regency' in the strict sense covers the years from 1811 to 1820 but as far as antiques and architecture are concerned it is used to cover the three decades from 1800 to 1830, a period which saw a complete change in furniture design. It became more decorative and was greatly influenced by the new 'Empire' style in France which, in turn, was inspired by the designs of ancient Greece and Egypt.

By 1830, the use of machinery for making furniture was increasing and the number of first-class craftsmen steadily declined. In wealthier Victorian times the size of furniture often seemed to reflect social status. Carving returned with a vengeance and was often pretentious, fussy and ornate. Much of the grace that had been achieved in the previous 100 years was lost. There were, nevertheless, some distinctive styles in domestic furniture which emerged as a result of the great emphasis placed on comfort. The framework of the armchair and sofa had to lend itself to the padding of the arms and backs. Outlines became rounded and square backs disappeared. Over the same period, veneering and inlay virtually disappeared and ornamentation was restricted to the carving of solid wood, usually mahogany, rosewood or walnut. In general metal handles on furniture were giving way to wooden ones.

In the Edwardian period which followed, some of the vulgarity of the previous hundred years seems to have been recognized and the cabinet-makers spent much of the time copying the eighteenth-century designs of Sheraton, often quite well. This is why the words 'Sheraton-style china cabinet' so often appear in auction sale catalogues; many were made in Edwardian times.

Materials readily available for making furniture varied from period to period and fashions also played a part. Some timbers were cut from our own British trees, others were imported from all parts of the world. Only those people closely associated with the antique furniture trade, or who work constantly with timber of all kinds, are likely to be able to recognize the many woods that have been employed over the years. But most people can soon learn to identify those which have been widely used.

The earliest furniture was made of oak drawn mainly from the woodlands which, in Tudor and Stuart times, extended more widely over the lowland areas of Britain than they do now. It is a coarse-grained, heavy wood noted for its strength. It has a great colour range and over the years develops a fine natural sheen or patina from polishing and constant use. It also darkens with age and is less subject to woodworm than many other woods. In late Stuart times, a good deal of oak was either japanned or else coated with several layers of varnish and then polished. This protected the oak which was otherwise liable to warp from changes of humidity and temperature.

Towards the end of the seventeenth century, in Restoration times, walnut became very popular for making furniture. Much of it came from England – a pale brown wood with dark veining – but the severe winter of 1709 destroyed many walnut trees and supplies had to be supplemented by considerable imports from France. Walnut had advantages over oak; the closer grain enabled craftsmen to produce a smoother finish to their work; moreover walnut is slightly softer and lighter than oak and the varied direction of grain makes it easier to work. It soon became so much in demand that supplies were insufficient and craftsmen began to use veneers of walnut, thin sheets of the wood glued to a carcase made of a cheaper and often softer wood, such as pine. Early in the eighteenth century France stopped her exports of walnut and supplies of a darker walnut were brought in from the eastern parts of America. The very definite whirled graining of some walnut was used to advantage. This oyster-shell veneering was very popular during the William and Mary period (Illus. 1). The growth rings in each of the pieces of applied veneer look very like the concentric circular layers seen on oyster shells. Plain walnut furniture of the early eighteenth century was often decorated with patterns made from different coloured woods and set into the piece. This is known as inlay: an example is shown in Illus. 2. This method of decorating furniture grew in popularity as the years passed and reached perfection in French furniture (Illus. 3).

In the early eighteenth century a new imported wood

was being tried – mahogany. *The Book of Trees* (1852)
tells the story of how it came into use.

A London physician of the name of Gibbon had a
brother the captain of a West India ship. On his return
to England he had several logs of mahogany on board
his vessel for the purpose of ballast, and, as his brother
was at that time employed in a building project, he
made him a present of the wood, supposing it might be
useful; his carpenter, however, cast it on one side, ob-
serving that it was of too hard a nature to be worked.
Some time after, Mrs Gibbon being in want of a box to
hold candles, the cabinet-maker was directed to make
it of this same wood; he, in his turn, made the same
objection as the carpenter, and declared that it spoilt
his tools. Being urged, however, to make another
trial, he at length succeeded; and when the box was
polished, the beautiful colour of its grain was so apparent and novel that it became an object of great curiosity, and attracted the notice, among others, of the
Duchess of Buckingham, for whom a bureau was made
of the same material.

By about 1730, much fine-quality mahogany was being
brought into Britain, mainly from Jamaica. It has a rich,
reddish-brown colour and a fine, straight grain and is an
extremely strong wood for making veneers. Its fineness of
grain made it particularly well suited to the highly-pol-
ished surfaces which were being demanded, while the size
of the trees provided wide boards especially suitable for
tabletops. In early Georgian times it was used for making
solid furniture, and replaced walnut as the chief wood. By
the reign of George III it was being used for fine veneering.

As the supplies of mahogany from Jamaica began to
run out, new sources were tapped in San Domingo and

Cuba. This wood is known in the trade as Spanish mahogany. Still later, supplies came from Honduras but this timber, which grows on the flat, marshy coastlands, is lighter and looser in texture than the timber from the mountainous West Indian islands, though easier to work. The trained eye can distinguish between the various types of mahogany.

From about 1760 the light, golden-coloured satinwood which, as its name suggests, has a sheen like satin, gradually came into fashion. Some came from the West Indies, some from the East Indies. Both varieties were used for all forms of inlay decoration. Satinwood was also widely used for cross-banding since the light colour made an agreeable contrast to the reddish browns of mahogany.

Rosewood – a deep brown wood with definite darker stripes running through it – first came in towards the end of the seventeenth century but lent itself particularly to the flamboyant furniture of the Regency period, when it was widely used for solid work and veneering. It continued to find favour in Victorian times. Rosewood gets its name from the pleasing, fragrant aroma it gives off while being worked.

Zebra wood, used mainly between 1780 and 1820, is rather similar to rosewood in appearance, but the contrast between the stripes and the ground colour is stronger.

Ebony is a hard, black wood usually used for inlay work or for smaller pieces of furniture, though some was used for larger pieces during the late seventeenth century. Softer, close-grained woods were often stained black or 'ebonized' to represent ebony, but they can usually be detected by their lighter weight.

Woods such as ash, beech, yew, elm and chestnut were used a great deal during the seventeenth, eighteenth and nineteenth centuries as they rather resembled oak in general appearance but were easier to work. These woods

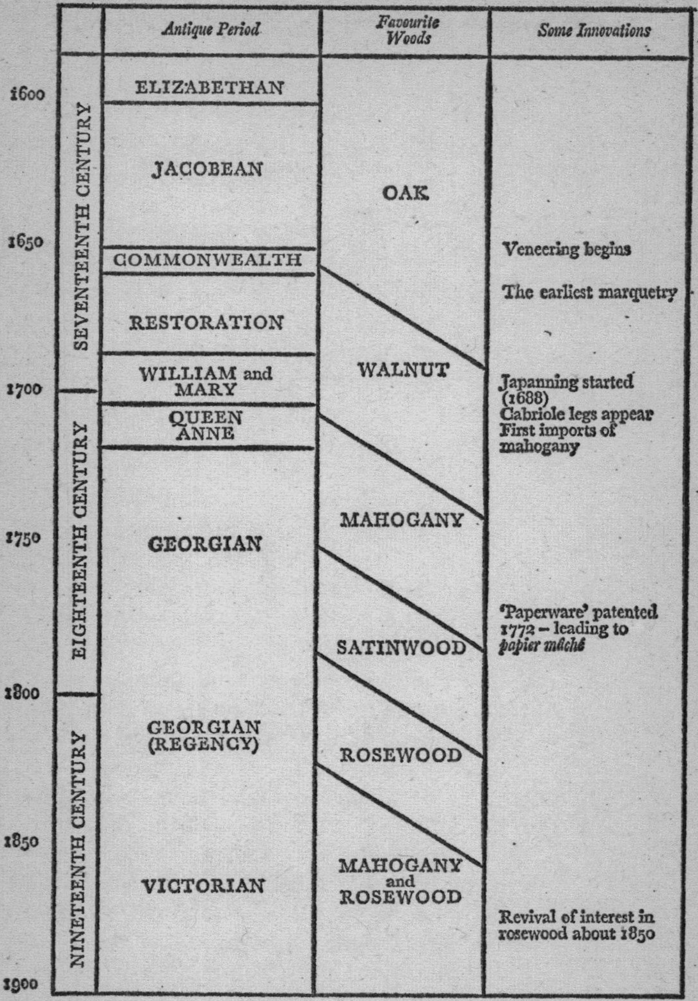

		Antique Period	Favourite Woods	Some Innovations
1600	SEVENTEENTH CENTURY	ELIZABETHAN	OAK	
		JACOBEAN		
1650		COMMONWEALTH		Veneering begins
				The earliest marquetry
		RESTORATION		
1700		WILLIAM and MARY	WALNUT	Japanning started (1688)
	EIGHTEENTH CENTURY	QUEEN ANNE		Cabriole legs appear First imports of mahogany
1750		GEORGIAN	MAHOGANY	
			SATINWOOD	'Paperware' patented 1772 – leading to *papier mâché*
1800		GEORGIAN (REGENCY)	ROSEWOOD	
1850	NINETEENTH CENTURY	VICTORIAN	MAHOGANY and ROSEWOOD	
1900				Revival of interest in rosewood about 1850

Figure 2   THE FAVOURITE WOODS FOR FURNITURE-MAKING

were used particularly by country craftsmen but they are prone to woodworm. You will find, however, that woodworm detracts little from the value of really good early country furniture.

Another material was used from the second half of the eighteenth century as an alternative to wood for making furniture, particularly smaller items such as tea caddies, spill holders and trays. This is now generally known as *papier mâché*, though an early form invented by Henry Clay in 1772 should strictly be referred to as paper-ware.

Papier mâché was made from layers of rags or paper soaked in an adhesive mixture of such materials as flour, size or glue. The pulped paper was then pressed into a metal mould, a layer at a time, and baked. The final product could be worked like wood and was so strong that even chairs could be made from it. The surface was covered with black lacquer, which was then polished by hand. *Papier mâché* articles were usually decorated with coloured or gilded floral designs or landscapes. A number of pieces were inlaid with mother-of-pearl. It is generally agreed that some of the best-quality *papier mâché* was made by Jennens and Bettridge between about 1820 and 1850, but only a few pieces bear a maker's name.

The quality of antique furniture depends on its design, the quality of the wood, and the standard of the workmanship. The finest pieces tend to be associated with the name of a designer, a craftsman, or a particular workshop which settled for nothing but the best. During the eighteenth century designs were not protected by copyright and they could therefore be copied freely. As a result, a number of well-known 'styles' were established, based on the work of the best designers. Anyone developing an interest in antiques must aim to recognize these, although the actual work of the best designers and craftsmen is beyond the means of the average person buying for the home.

In the eighteenth and early nineteenth century the style of many pieces was set by one of the designers of the period – men such as William Kent, Thomas Chippendale, Robert Adam, George Hepplewhite, Thomas Sheraton and Thomas Hope. Their designs became widely popular because they were published in book form and could be copied by fine cabinet-makers and by small firms all over the country.

Kent, who spent some time in Italy studying painting, was not only a furniture designer but artist, architect and landscape designer as well. His furniture in the 1730s was solid in appearance with cabriole legs and much decoration with acanthus leaves and gilding. He also used carved eagles and dolphins. Some of his designs were published in 1744 in a book by Vardy called *Designs of Inigo Jones and Kent*.

Chippendale was a Yorkshireman whose father was a carpenter, but it is known that by the time he was thirty years of age he was married and working in London. He took a shop in Long Acre and later acquired premises in St Martin's Lane. Although he already had an established business reputation as a maker of furniture, his real influence dates from 1754 when he issued 150 designs in *The Gentleman and Cabinet-maker's Director*, some of which were by cabinet-makers who worked for him. Chippendale had a fine eye for proportion and adapted many of the earlier and heavy Georgian designs to produce furniture – mainly in mahogany – which was lighter and more graceful but at the same time just as strong. His tables and chairs often have ball and claw feet on cabriole legs. His chairs often have carved splats and the line of the top rail is usually curved or broken. Many people regard Chippendale as the finest of all furniture designers; contemporary cabinet-makers who used his designs to make their own pieces were responsible for the wide range of furniture known as 'Chippendale'.

Before Chippendale died in 1779 a new style was beginning to establish itself. This was associated with the
name of Robert Adam, son of a Scottish architect. He did
not make furniture himself but used his architectural
training and skill (which had been greatly influenced by
travel in Italy and France) to initiate designs derived
from classical styles. The trend away from the heaviness
of early Georgian furniture started by Chippendale was
carried much further by Adam. Everything became
lighter and more elegant; the ornamentation had a new
delicate beauty and in due course the material used
changed from mahogany to lighter woods such as beech
painted in white or soft greens and blues. Adam's designs
were issued in *Works in Architecture* which was prepared
in collaboration with his brother, James, and started pub-
lication in 1773.

Meanwhile, a well-known cabinet-maker, George Hepplewhite, was working on his own designs in a London
workshop, designs which were to gain little popularity in
his lifetime. They were not particularly original; he was
mainly interested in making chairs and these were based
on Chippendale's designs with the splats and the legs
fined down to produce a lighter style. He loved the graceful line and made great use of the curve, introducing oval,
heart-shaped and shield-shaped backs. He died in 1786
but two years later his widow published his *Cabinet-
maker and Upholsterer's Guide* which ran through three
editions in a few years. This is when Hepplewhite's
influence really began and it continued until roughly
1800. It is interesting to note that he was the first designer
to use the Prince of Wales' feathers as a decorative motif
on furniture.

While Robert Adam was still alive, a third influence
came into play. Thomas Sheraton who, although he had
some training as a cabinet-maker, had no workshop of his
own, brought out some fine new designs in *The Cabinet-*

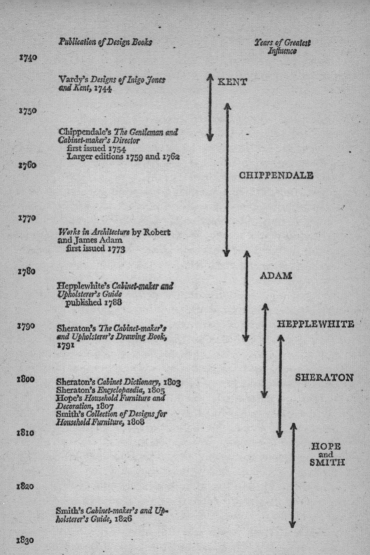

1740

Vardy's *Designs of Inigo Jones and Kent*, 1744

KENT

1750

Chippendale's *The Gentleman and Cabinet-maker's Director*
   first issued 1754
     Larger editions 1759 and 1762

1760

CHIPPENDALE

1770

Works in Architecture by Robert and James Adam
   first issued 1773

1780

ADAM

Hepplewhite's *Cabinet-maker and Upholsterer's Guide*
   published 1788

1790

HEPPLEWHITE

Sheraton's *The Cabinet-maker's and Upholsterer's Drawing Book*, 1791

1800

SHERATON

Sheraton's *Cabinet Dictionary*, 1803
Sheraton's *Encyclopaedia*, 1805
Hope's *Household Furniture and Decoration*, 1807
Smith's *Collection of Designs for Household Furniture*, 1808

1810

HOPE and SMITH

1820

Smith's *Cabinet-maker's and Up-holsterer's Guide*, 1826

1830

Figure 3   CABINET-MAKERS AND DESIGNERS OF THE GEORGIAN PERIOD

maker's and Upholsterer's Drawing Book in 1791. His designs tend to be 'straight and narrow'. He damned Chippendale's work as out-of-date and reacted against the use of the curve. There is a severe look about Sheraton chairs when compared with earlier designs. But he rejoiced in detail and much Sheraton furniture has fine veneering with satinwood and sycamore, and beautiful inlay work using satinwood, tulipwood and many other carefully-chosen materials.

Sheraton followed his first book with a *Cabinet Dictionary* (1803) and a *Cabinet-maker, Upholsterer and General Artist's Encyclopaedia* (1805). He died in 1806.

Already the influence of the French Empire style was having its effect on this side of the Channel, based as it was on the earlier styles of Greece and Rome and on the antiquities of Egypt. Thomas Hope, who came from a Dutch banking family, had travelled widely in Mediterranean countries. This, and his friendship with the French architect, Percier, led him to work on classical styles for the fashionable English market. In 1807, his *Household Furniture and Decoration* was published. Later, the Regency style became even more complicated: both Gothic and Oriental influences can be seen in the famous Brighton Pavilion. Unfortunately, many of Hope's designs for furniture paid too little attention to comfort and homeliness to satisfy many ordinary people. To meet the popular demand, they were often modified by the men who had to make and sell their goods. George Smith, a London furniture-maker, did this on a considerable scale and issued his own collection of designs for *Household Furniture and Interior Decoration* in 1808. He was certainly influenced by Hope but he also studied the work of Augustus Welby Pugin, the architect, who was anxious to revive the Gothic style. George Smith's second book, *The Cabinet-maker's and Upholsterer's Guide* published in 1826, reveals the influence of Pugin's ideas.

BUYING FURNITURE

Much of the fine furniture made by early craftsmen has lasted for generations and is now keenly sought. It often commands prices as high as those paid for articles made of precious metals such as silver. The value, of course, lies in the workmanship and because the basic material used in furniture – mainly wood – is relatively cheap, it is a field in which there is a great deal of faking and open reproduction of earlier styles. Moreover, since furniture suffers greatly from wear and tear, comparatively little old furniture is in its original state: most pieces have had repair work of some kind done to them. This is why the expert studies pieces with such great care. He will probably start by making a quick assessment at a glance but before he will commit himself to a certain identification he will open cupboards, pull out drawers, look carefully at handles and hinges and scrutinize the piece in detail and from every angle.

What does one need to know about antique furniture? The period during which it was made, the 'style', and the type of wood used. When this identification has been made it should be possible to assess its value, which will depend to a great extent on the craftsmanship and the condition. It is also helpful to know how articles have been made because methods of construction varied according to the practice of the time and the tools available to the craftsmen.

The amount of furniture actually made by the great designers and cabinet-makers of the eighteenth century, or by the craftsmen and apprentices in their workshops, must be very small indeed, though it is very occasionally possible to identify a piece when it is signed. It was their designs which were significant and the circulation of their design books, which were used by small firms all over the

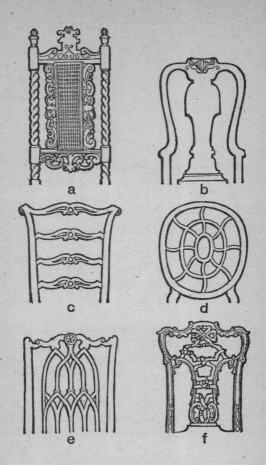

Figure 4   CHAIR BACKS

(*a*) Caning, carving and spiral twist (Stuart, second half seventeenth century)
(*b*) Solid Splat (Queen Anne and early Georgian)
(*c*) Ladder Back (Chippendale, mid-eighteenth century)
(*d*) Wheel Back (Hepplewhite, late eighteenth century)
(*e*) Gothic (Chippendale, mid-eighteenth century)
(*f*) Ribband Back (Chippendale, mid-eighteenth century)

country, led to the wide popularity of their styles. Much
of this early furniture consists of so-called 'country-made'
pieces. Wealthier people could afford the expensive work
turned out by the finest craftsmen using the very best
materials but this was beyond the means of many country
people who, instead, bought from small carpenters who
tried to be in the fashion by copying the work of the
London designers. Country-made pieces are noted for
their simplicity, and lack the finish of the finer pieces.
The woods used were very often cheaper and there was
relatively little carving, partly because this took time and
added to the cost, and partly because country craftsmen
seldom had the skill to do this kind of work. Nevertheless,
much country furniture is good and attractive and may
often be obtained at a reasonable price.

The homes of the wealthy in the eighteenth and nineteenth centuries were larger than houses are today and
furniture, too, tended to be larger. Small antique pieces
which will fit readily into the modern home are therefore
in greater demand and are consequently more expensive.
Bureaux, chests-of-drawers and side tables are usually
much less desirable if they are more than about 3 ft
wide.

Because of the demand for small furniture, many larger pieces have been cut down and reassembled. This
should be watched for. If a suspect piece has drawers,
look for the marks where the handles may originally have
been attached. If the drawer front has been cut down, the
handles will have been moved inwards to retain the
balance. Look also at the drawer runners, which should
show considerable signs of wear in an old piece of furniture as the result of years of pushing and pulling out.
Made-up tables are relatively common. These may
well have legs from one period married to the top from
another.

Victorian furniture, which a few years ago was in little

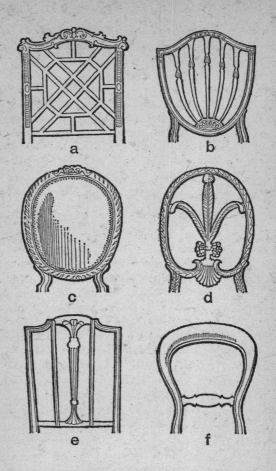

Figure 5 MORE CHAIR BACKS

(a) Chinese (Chippendale, mid-eighteenth century)
(b) Shield Back (Hepplewhite, late eighteenth century)
(c) Stuffed Oval (Adam, late eighteenth century)
(d) Prince of Wales Plumes (Hepplewhite, late eighteenth century)
(e) Sheraton (late eighteenth century)
(f) Balloon Back (Victorian, mid-nineteenth century)

demand, is now commanding quite high prices. Much of it is full of character and can look charming in the right setting. Given time to seek out the right pieces, it is certainly possible to furnish a home with nineteenth-century furniture for little more than it would cost to equip it with the modern, mass-produced article. Even good-quality Edwardian furniture is increasing in price: in a recent auction sale a mahogany display cabinet, banded in satinwood, fetched £122. But this was not an 'antique'. We now consider a number of articles which are older but still relatively inexpensive.

Tables

These are always useful for a variety of purposes, and there is a wide selection to choose from. It is fair to say that, on the whole, the heavier a table is, the cheaper it is. For this reason, quite early country-made oak tables are worth looking for, especially the seventeenth-century, Jacobean-style, gate-legged table which was still made in large numbers well into the eighteenth century. Look for tenon and mortice joints with dowel pins. In early oak furniture the dowel pins are usually irregular in shape – never exactly circular. The turned legs of an old table will differ very slightly if you examine them closely, unlike the precision machine-made examples current today. The stretchers will normally show signs of wear where people have rested their feet on them but they should nevertheless show a good patina. Prices of such tables, however, are rising rapidly. Round tables with single pillars and three legs are commoner and cheaper. They have been made at all periods, especially in oak and mahogany. The single pillars allow more seating and more knee room. These tables usually tilt: there is a catch below the top which, when released, allows the top to be tipped up vertically so that the table may be placed against a wall. If the tops are large, this looks rather ugly; consequently, sought-after examples tend to be small. The pillars of these tables are usually turned, though some are fluted or writhen (twisted). The legs may vary from the sabre of the Regency period to the legs with 'knees' of the Victorian period. In general, the more definite the 'knee' the later in Victoria's reign the table was made.

Two- or three-pillar dining tables are much sought after but are generally expensive. Many Victorian dining tables had extra leaves which were fastened into place with brass clips at the sides.

Several other types of table of the Victorian period are attractive and have many uses. Small card tables were often made which would either stand against a wall or open out to a green baize top measuring about 3 ft by 3 ft 6 ins. They were often made in pairs, one of which had a plain polished interior which could be used as a tea table.

Pembroke tables have flaps hanging on each of the longer sides which can be opened up to form quite a large dining table. They usually have a long shallow drawer at one end, the other end having a matching 'dummy' drawer.

Sofa tables were a direct invention of the Regency period, and were so-called because of their normal position in the house – behind the sofa which stood in the middle of the room. These tables have a flap which drops on each of the two shorter sides. Usually the long side contains drawers. However, there are sometimes two drawers to one side with 'dummy' drawers on the back; sometimes one drawer and a 'dummy' on each side. Unfortunately, many such tables in Victorian times were rather heavy and clumsy.

Sutherland tables are reputed to have been named after the Duchess of Sutherland who popularized the design during the Victorian period. These are small flap tables normally about 3 ft long by 2 ft wide when in the open position. The flaps are supported by legs which pull out in the same way as a gate-leg table and when folded down they take up very little room. They are usually quite low and are ideal tables for coffee or cards.

Wine tables were often placed around a room within comfortable reach of easy-chairs so that books or drinks could be placed on them. They are sometimes known as pedestal or tripod tables and, as these names imply, they had a single column leg and a small round top, usually 1 ft to 2 ft in diameter, and three legs.

Chairs

Dining-room chairs were made in sets – as they are today – and are valued as such. A set of six matching chairs might, for example, fetch £80, whereas as single chairs they might only be worth about £5 or £6 each. Some early Victorian dining-room chairs can be very attractive. Following the Regency period in 1830, most chairs retained the broad yoke-rail back which extended beyond the uprights which were joined lower down by a narrower horizontal splat, nearly always carved. The front legs were straight and either turned or fluted. The seats were padded. Within a few years the broad yoke-rail began to disappear and chairs were made in which the uprights and the back follow a continuous curve which became more pronounced as the years passed. By 1845, the full-blown balloon-back chair was common.

Mother and Father chairs were very popular during the Victorian period. Father chairs are the large, upholstered, easy-chairs with arms; the Mother chair is a smaller matching chair, often without arms. They can be bought separately and matched later, as many of the designs were standard.

The frames of these delightful chairs are usually made

of mahogany, rosewood or beech. Examine beech pieces with great care. Beech is a softer and cheaper wood very subject to woodworm. Check that the joints are sound, paying particular attention to the point where the back legs join the chair and the point where the arms of the 'Father' chair join. The upholstery is often 'button-backed'. If you buy these chairs intending to have them re-upholstered, remember that labour alone on such a job can be costly.

Victorian sofas were the equivalent of the modern settee. These varied enormously in size and, as a rule, it is safe to say that the larger they are the more comfortable they are likely to be. The small salon-type sofa with a very upright back may have been suitable for the postures of the period, but is hardly so for relaxing. Watch out for those which have been cut down from large settees, a slice having been taken from the middle and the two ends re-joined.

Chest-of-Drawers

Victorian chests-of-drawers are usually very large; they seemed to believe in the old saying 'the bigger the better'. The craftsmanship was superb and the woods excellent. If you are lucky enough to find a smaller one, you will have a nice-looking, durable piece of furniture. Many had bow fronts which give a graceful appearance. Unfortunately, the Victorians were very fond of large wooden handles which project into the room and are a constant cause of bumps and bruises. These have often been removed and replaced by brass handles.

It is useful to know that in most eighteenth-century furniture made before 1730 the grain in the wood in the bottom of the drawer runs from back to front. From 1730 to 1830, it was made to run from side to side and from about 1810 a rounded beading was usually inserted along

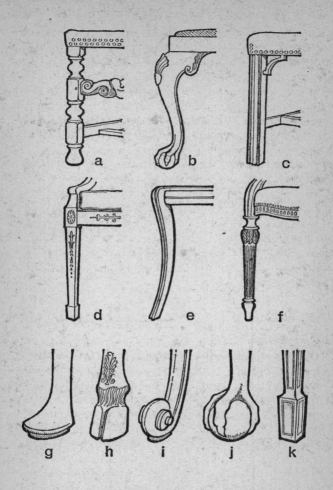

Figure 6   CHAIR LEGS AND FEET

Legs: (*a*) Turned; (*b*) Cabriole; (*c*) Moulded; (*d*) Tapered; (*e*) Sabre; (*f*) Turned and Fluted

Feet: (*g*) Pad; (*h*) Hoof; (*i*) Scroll; (*j*) Claw and Ball; (*k*) Spade or Peg

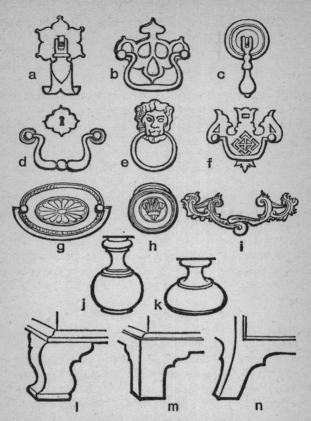

Figure 7 FURNITURE MOUNTS AND
SUPPORTS

Mounts: (*a*) Axe Drop (mid-seventeenth century); (*b*) Swan Neck
with shaped pierced plate (early eighteenth century); (*c*) Pear Drop
(late seventeenth century); (*d*) Swan Neck (Queen Anne); (*e*) Lion
Mask (Regency); (*f*) Pierced back plate with Chinese influence
(mid-eighteenth century); (*g*) Neo-classical (Adam); (*h*) Prince of
Wales plumes (late eighteenth century); (*i*) French Rococo (mid-
eighteenth century)
Supports: (*j*) Ball; (*k*) Bun; (*l*) Ogee; (*m*) Bracket; (*n*) Splayed
Bracket

each inside bottom edge of the drawers so that dust would not collect in the crevices.

Desks

Most Victorian desks and bureaux were so large that they are seldom suitable for the small modern home, but from this period come some of the most delightful small or ladies' desks, generally known as davenports. The name derives from the fact that the first customer to order one from Gillow of Lancaster was a Captain Davenport. They had a great appeal to ladies of late Regency and Victorian days, who were great writers of notes, letters and formal invitations. The whole of one side of a davenport is usually devoted to drawers, with compartments inside for storing stationery and writing materials. Those with good interior fittings are worth more money. Davenports are very useful pieces of furniture: they are not only small and decorative but contain a great deal of valuable storage space.

'What nots'

These normally consist of four turned posts, usually on castors, which support a series of shelves and sometimes a shallow drawer. They were used for ornaments, photographs and knick-knacks and first appeared in Regency times. In Victorian days, few houses were without them. They can still be bought quite reasonably if, indeed, you have any desire for one. They can be very useful as display units or magazine stands or, if you are lucky enough to find one large enough, strong enough and low enough, as a television table.

Mirrors

Mirrors are an essential part of any home and antique mirrors are usually most attractive. The mirrored glass is generally referred to as the plate. Most frames are of wood, though there are some in ceramic frames and occasionally in a metal frame. In some early mirrors the reflecting part was made of highly polished metal.

In the second half of the seventeenth century in Britain, mirrors were usually rectangular and relatively small, as no technique had been discovered for mirroring large sheets of glass. The workshop which first succeeded in doing so was the Duke of Buckingham's Glassworks, Vauxhall, London. In the early eighteenth century this opened up a new range of possibilities for the mirror-maker and extremely large mirrors were often made, sometimes covering large portions of a wall. The glass or plate in such early mirrors is usually quite thin. The thickness of a mirror glass can be determined by holding a pointed object against the surface of the glass and noting the distance between the point and the reflection of the point. Most old plate has discoloured over the years and has a distinct blue-green or grey-green tinge and a mottled effect which gives a mildewed appearance. Bevelled glass in mirrors was popular during the reign of Queen Anne. Because the glass was so thin the bevels are usually broad and shallow. It was often set in plain wooden frames veneered with strips of walnut and edged with gilded plaster work (Illus. 10). The most important part of an old mirror is, of course, the frame, though it is always more valuable if it contains the original plate in reasonably good condition. Carved wood gilded frames appear to be the most popular and heading the list are those designed by Chippendale in the Chinese taste. Gilt frames were plentiful during the nineteenth century but were cheaply made of plaster shaped to look like carved wood and then gilded. It is sometimes difficult to distinguish between gilded wood and plaster. To do so, take a pin and press it slowly but firmly into a high point of relief in the frame. Then, holding the pin by its head, slowly pull. If the pin comes out with little or no effort it is plaster; if it needs a little tug to remove it, then it is wood. Do remember, however, that most of the plaster work was built up on a wooden base, so try the pin test in several different places.

Many carved wood picture frames today pose as mirror frames. Among these is a particular type of carved wood frame which was very common in Italy during the late eighteenth and early nineteenth century. These, though desirable, are not as valuable as those made in this country. They can be distinguished by their florid, curling carved leaves; they are light in weight for their size and the gilding has a distinctly green tinge.

In the eighteenth century, a plaster-like substance made of a mixture of chalk and size was used for decorating woodwork. This is known as gesso work and it is often difficult for an amateur to distinguish between this and nineteenth-century plasterwork. In gesso, the 'plaster' is very thin; in plaster work it is completely solid.

Many early mirrors have candles fitted to them. This served two purposes. The candles illuminated the face of the person using the mirror and the light was reflected by the mirror into the room.

During the William and Mary period, mirrors were usually mounted in thick rectangular frames veneered with tortoiseshell. Early Georgian mirrors had simple wooden frames veneered with walnut and wall mirrors were also set in flat-shaped wooden plaques which were decorated with delicate, gilded scrolls of gesso.

During the Regency period, circular convex mirrors were popular. These were decorated with small, gilded, wooden balls round the interior rim of the bulky, round, wooden frame and were often surmounted by a gilded and carved wooden eagle. It is said that these were often hung above a sideboard or serving table at the end of a dining-room so that a butler could keep an eye on the requirements of the diners without actually facing them. Modern reproductions of this type of mirror abound.

Here are some of the types of antique mirror you may come across in shops or auction rooms.

A Cheval glass was a long, narrow mirror supported on a stand in such a way that the mirror could be tilted to give a full-length view.

A Mantel mirror or overmantel consisted of a single, large mirror or sometimes a series of mirrors fixed to the wall above the fireplace. They were an essential item of home furnishing in Georgian and Victorian times.

A Pier glass was a mirror hung on the wall between windows, with a side table matching the frame standing beneath.

Toilet or dressing mirrors were swinging mirrors supported between two uprights on a base which rather resembled a small bureau with little drawers for trinkets, etc. They first appeared during the late seventeenth century and were made right through Georgian times. Sheraton dressing mirrors are still extremely popular and command quite high prices with their delicate, often shield-shaped mirrors and their shallow, three-drawer box-stands. These have been reproduced time and time again. When buying a toilet mirror, look for repaired or replaced uprights: these are the parts most likely to have been broken.

THE CARE OF FURNITURE

It is easy in the sudden burst of enthusiasm which so often comes with a new purchase to start on a cleaning or repairing operation without sufficient consideration of what the result of such action may be. It is useful, therefore, to sound a note of warning in order to focus attention on the condition of what you may hope to buy and to give a word of advice on how best to treat the antiques you do buy.

It can generally be said that minor repairs to furniture detract little from the value provided they have been done expertly by a skilled craftsman. Nor does the presence of a few woodworm holes, particularly in an unseen place, completely ruin a piece, provided the damage has not gone too far and the piece has been, or can be, properly treated. However, if the activity has been so great that the wood in any place has become soft and spongy, leave the piece alone unless it is so desirable as to warrant an expensive repair.

It is unwise to get out the wax furniture polish in order to give a piece of furniture a high sheen. Years of use have probably given it a natural patina and this can easily be lost beneath a greasy film. Nothing beats old-fashioned 'elbow grease'. It is surprising how quickly an apparently dull surface on old furniture will respond to a good rub with a soft cloth.

Veneered furniture needs special care because under certain conditions the veneer 'lifts' or 'bubbles'. This is most likely to happen if the furniture is exposed to strong sunlight near a window, or if it is left in centrally-heated rooms without humidifiers. Heat from either source can also cause warping, which will cost a great deal of money to put right. So if you have central heating, think twice before investing in expensive, veneered furniture.

Some solid furniture, especially oak, can be cleaned by washing it gently with a damp cloth which has been soaked in warm water to which a little vinegar has been added. It can then be polished with a cloth on which a few drops of raw linseed oil have been sprinkled. Never have anything to do with varnish. Some furniture has been treated with varnish but such pieces are of little interest to the antique collector even if the price is low. It is true that varnish can be removed but it is a lengthy and expensive process which also involves repolishing and the resulting surface bears no comparison with the patina acquired by age.

Stain should never be used on antique furniture. Any presence of staining on the basic framework of a piece of furniture usually indicates the replacement of some part, or that the piece is a reproduction.

CHAPTER THREE

CLOCKS, WATCHES AND BAROMETERS

O LD clocks can look very attractive in the modern home, but without some knowledge of the working they are tricky things to buy, particularly at auction sales. Although they may look sound and appear to be in working order, it is difficult for the amateur to tell whether parts of the movement have been replaced or modernized. If they have, such clocks are much less valuable than a genuine clock in its original condition. A clock or watch which is not in working order is seldom a good buy: the cost of repairs can be very high. To appreciate the value of old clocks it is essential to understand the various movements that have been used and developed over the centuries. This will come with experience and personal study. As with all antiques there is more to it than meets the eye.

Most old clocks fall into one of the following groups: lantern, bracket, long-case, mantel, ormolu and carriage.

Lantern Clocks

These are so called because they are similar in shape to an old lantern. They were originally made during the early seventeenth century but have been much copied. They were of brass and have a large bell above the working parts. Some of these were called 'bird-cage clocks' as the shape was similar to that of a bird cage. Another word used is 'Cromwellian'. There were doors on each side to give access to the movement.

Bracket Clocks

Bracket clocks were so called because they rested on brackets mounted on the wall, though very few exist today with their original brackets. They are usually much larger than modern clocks and the more desirable ones have pull winds. This was a cord with an ivory or wooden knob which, when pulled, wound the mechanism. Bracket clocks usually had a wooden case with brass or ormolu mounts, with a carrying handle at the top. The sides were often of fretted metal panels backed with coloured silk. Bracket clocks were common in late Georgian and Regency times.

Long-Case Clocks

The first long-case clocks in this country were made in the seventeenth century and they were still being made by country craftsmen when Victoria came to the throne. It is not surprising therefore that there is hardly an antique shop in the country without a long-case or 'grandfather' clock for sale. Although large numbers were made, many of them are of little value. Those that fetch high prices are either very early examples, or were made by one of the few select clockmakers such as Thomas Tompion or Daniel Quare, whose workmanship was of the very highest quality. Most of these worked in London, so grandfather clocks made in the provinces are less likely to be of great value. As a general rule, old long-case clocks should have brass dials ten inches or less in diameter in order to have interest for the serious collector. Old clocks with single hands (ie, the hour hand) are interesting. Many people dismiss them as having a hand missing but it is usually possible to tell by looking at the arbor or axle on which the hand is mounted to see whether there has ever been provision for another hand. One-handed clocks were made throughout the seventeenth century.

Clocks with painted dials (usually on wood or iron) followed the etched and silvered brass dials of the mid-seventeenth century. More often than not they are of no great value.

The style of the wooden cases usually corresponds to the style of furniture of the period and, as with furniture, the smaller the clock the greater the demand and the more valuable it is likely to be. 'Grandmother' clocks, which are less than 6 ft in height, are much easier to accommodate in the modern home than the very large grandfather clocks.

When buying an old grandfather clock, make sure that it has not been rehoused in a new case as this detracts greatly from its value. Good-quality clocks sometimes have a brass plate decorated with an etched design at the back of the clock movement. When the lead weights are enclosed in a copper sheath it is often a sign of quality manufacture.

It is important that all pendulum clocks should be placed on a level surface in a position where the pendulum swings exactly the same distance from the vertical on both sides. Slight variations from such a position will cause the clock to gain or lose, or even to stop.

Mantel Clocks

These clocks, as their name implies, stood on the mantelshelf. They were first in use during the mid-seventeenth century and, like bracket clocks, were popular because they could be moved easily from place to place without upsetting the delicate balance of the pendulum. In Regency and Victorian times, mantel clocks were made with matching side pieces – decorative ornaments which matched the style of the clock and which stood on either side of it. The whole set was known as a *garniture-de-cheminée* and often included candlesticks, urns or vases: most of the side pieces have by now been detached from the clock sets and disposed of separately.

Ormolu Clocks

Ormolu is gilded brass or bronze, and clocks encased in this material are known as ormolu clocks. They usually rest on a base from which rise decorative mounts with figures or animals, all of the same material. These clocks were made in large numbers in France during the Empire period and are greatly valued. They are usually wound from the face. Many of them have small porcelain plaques inset, decorated with colourful scenes in enamel. These were generally referred to as Sèvres plaques, though most of them were certainly not made there.

Owing to the popularity of French ormolu clocks in the nineteenth century, manufacturers in England and France began to flood the market with cheap copies made from the soft base metal known as spelter, which was moulded and then covered with a thin layer of gilt. They can easily be recognized as they are relatively light in weight. The metal bends easily and is soft when filed. The gilt often bubbled, leaving small blisters.

Carriage Clocks

These clocks were originally designed to be carried when travelling. They were kept in specially made leather cases with a sliding panel which could be lifted to reveal the face. Some of these clocks had an added refinement – a button on the top which, when pressed, operated a mechanism which chimed the nearest hour. This made it possible for travellers to tell the approximate time in the dark. Decorative carriage clocks with thin glass sides and ormolu or brass framework are extremely popular and are still made today. Many of them have French movements which were cased by English clockmakers. The more intricate the workmanship of the case and the more refinements such as repeat, alarm and chime included in it, the more expensive the clock will be.

Watches

Old silver and gold watches are often found among family heirlooms. Few of them are of any great value unless, of course, they were made by famous makers. Even fine old Georgian silver pocket watches are little sought after and rarely fetch more than a few pounds. Many dealers still break these watches up and keep only the silver case to be sold for its value as scrap. It is worth remembering that these watches in good working order can be mounted on stands and used as clocks.

Barometers

Barometers appear to have been invented about the middle of the seventeenth century. A simple laboratory barometer consisted of a long glass tube with the open lower end immersed in a dish of mercury. Variations in the atmospheric pressure on the surface of the mercury in the dish forced the level in the tube to go up or down. Changes in level were measured against a scale at the side of the tube which gave some guide to weather conditions.

It was from this simple piece of apparatus that stick or cistern barometers developed, and they were still popular well into the nineteenth century. But perhaps the best known and most attractive of all forms of barometer is the 'banjo' type in which the yard-long length of glass tube is curled about itself, eliminating the need for a long and often cumbersome case, and making it possible to have a circular dial. In the banjo barometer, a thermometer is usually included in the upright part of the case.

Unlike clocks, which tend to be judged largely on the quality of their movements, barometers are judged on the quality of their case. Some of our great cabinet-makers have designed barometer cases. Many Victorian barometers with plain unveneered cases, often of oak, can today be bought quite cheaply.

THE CARE OF CLOCKS AND BAROMETERS

Unless these are handled with great care on the journey from the saleroom or shop to your home, considerable damage can be done. Never move any pendulum clock without first removing the pendulum otherwise the delicate mechanism may be damaged. Always keep barometers upright, particularly the stick barometers, to prevent bubbles of air from entering the column of mercury. Above all, avoid jolting both clocks and barometers. Pack them round with soft materials when they are being transported and avoid rough routes if possible.

Ormolu clocks are often found to be dirty, but they can be cleaned provided the works are removed. Gently apply a mixture of equal parts of ammonia and water with a toothbrush – but do this in the open air because ammonia fumes can be overpowering. Wear rubber gloves to avoid staining the hands. The gold is revived incredibly quickly and once the tarnish has been removed the article should be washed thoroughly under running water and then thoroughly dried. The solution must not be allowed to touch anything but the ormolu: it will bleach woodwork and discolour enamel. Ormolu frames of mirrors may be cleaned in the same way, provided the mirror is removed before the operation.

CHAPTER FOUR

SILVER AND SHEFFIELD PLATE

SILVER has been used since the Middle Ages. Fortunately, it is easier to date and identify than furniture or porcelain since every British piece must, by law, have passed through an assay office to be assayed or tested. The assay office then marks the silver with its hall or assay mark (the name hallmark is commonly used for the assay mark because, in London, it is made in the Goldsmiths' and Silversmiths' Hall). The word 'hallmark' is now generally used to include several other marks that are made by the assay office at the same time. These enable us to learn a great deal about any particular piece of silver. On each piece it should normally be possible to find four marks (sometimes five) stamped on the metal (see Illus. 11). These are:

1. The *Hallmark*, or town mark, which indicates where the piece was assayed. For London, the hallmark is a leopard's head. This has been used since 1478, except for the years 1697 to 1719 when a particularly high standard of silver was introduced to stop silversmiths melting down silver coins of the realm. This is known as the Britannia period and a figure of Britannia was used as the mark. Between 1478 and 1821, the leopard's head bore a crown; after 1821 it was uncrowned. Britannia silver is still used today, mainly for presentation pieces.

In addition to the London Assay Office at Goldsmiths' Hall there are, or have been, assay offices in Birmingham, Chester, Dublin, Edinburgh, Exeter (1701–1883), Glasgow, Newcastle (1702–1884), Sheffield, York (1559–1857) and Norwich (1565–1702). Each has its own town mark.

2. The *Maker's Mark* consists in most cases of the initials of the silversmith who made the piece, though in Victorian times the mark was sometimes that of the firm which commissioned or sponsored the work. Most of the famous silversmiths worked in London and some identification handbooks list their initials and dates.

3. The *Date Letter* records the year when the piece was hallmarked at an assay office. It consists of a single letter of the alphabet in a particular style of print and shape of shield. These vary with each assay office, so it is first essential to identify the town where the piece was assayed. It is then possible to date the piece by referring to one of the many handbooks of marks.

4. The *Standard Mark,* which normally indicates that the silver is of sterling quality, is a lion *passant* (walking with the right forepaw raised). The only exception was during the Britannia period from 1697 to 1719, when a lion's head erased (the head and mane only) was the standard mark for the higher quality silver. The lion *passant* was not used on Scottish and Irish silver.

5. The *Sovereign's Head* is seen on silver assayed between 1784 and 1890. It indicates that the duty levied on silver during this period had been duly paid. Very small pieces were not liable to this duty.

Continental and foreign silver is imported into Britain and it is illegal for a dealer to sell such a piece as sterling silver unless it has been re-assayed on entry into this country. Any dealer selling a piece of foreign silver (which is usually of a lower standard than our own) which does not bear an English hallmark in addition to any mark of its country of origin is committing an offence if he sells it as sterling silver. The English hallmark will show if the silver is up to standard and also the year in which it entered this country. It is undoubtedly desirable that we should safeguard standards but it is sometimes sad to find that a piece of period foreign silver has had to be disfigured by the application of a modern English hall-mark.

As with furniture, silver had its fashionable craftsmen whose names have become well known because of the high quality of their work. Each of these famous silversmiths had a flair and style of his own. Experts who constantly see and handle silver get so accustomed to the 'feel' of pieces made by these craftsmen that they can often identify the maker without reference to the mark.

Most of the great names come from the eighteenth century. Perhaps the most famous is Paul de Lamerie who registered his work (LA with a crown above) in 1712. For some time after 1720 he continued to work in Britannia standard silver after the compulsory quality had dropped to sterling standard. His later work is noted for its figure engraving and applied decoration. By 1732, de Lamerie was using his second mark (PL with a crown above) on work made of the harder sterling standard silver.

Hester Bateman, whose work is particularly popular in the USA today, took over her husband's small business when he died and registered her mark (HB in script) in 1774. Her work was noted for its beaded borders, particularly on the edges of spoons and tableware, and on teapots, cream jugs, etc, and also for delicate piercing and a lively, bright-cut engraving which was designed to catch the light to give a sparkling appearance. Her sons joined her in the expanding business and became quality silversmiths in their own right. Her son Peter worked with his brother Jonathan (PBIB recorded in 1790), Jonathan's wife Ann (PBAB recorded 1791) and her son William (PBWB recorded 1805). It is worth noting that a lesser-known silversmith used the initials HB in script: so do not confuse this with the Hester Bateman mark.

Paul Storr was a fine silversmith who brought to his craft his own version of the classical revival. He first worked on his own in 1793 (Mark: PS or P.S.) and had his own workshop just off Piccadilly between 1795 and 1807, where he soon gained a great reputation. He executed commissions for the firm of Rundell, Bridge & Rundell who were appointed Jewellers, Gold and Silversmiths to the Crown in 1797. He joined the company in 1807 as their chief craftsman and his influence on the whole workshop must have been considerable. His great skill lay in his special ability to combine simplicity of line with an appearance of extravagance. Yet his designs never impeded usefulness.

BUYING SILVER

If you intend to buy silver or Sheffield plate it is obviously essential to be able to distinguish between them and also to be able to distinguish between Sheffield plate and more modern electro-plated articles. It is important, therefore, to equip yourself for the job. You would be well advised to set out with a nail file, a caustic pencil (which can be bought at any chemist's shop), a small Troy-weight spring balance for weighing the silver, a magnifying glass and a book of hallmarks. Some auctioneers will lend prospective buyers a balance on viewing days before sales of silver. It is pointless to weigh silver on kitchen scales which register Avoirdupois weight.

First, examine the hallmark. If it is difficult or impossible to decipher, then the piece is worth a good deal less than it would be if the hallmark were clear. So beware of indistinct hallmarks.

If you are examining a piece made in more than one part, a tankard with a lid for example, see that each part has a hallmark and that these marks match. Any piece which does not bear a hallmark should, by law, be taken to an assay office where it will be assayed and marked with the year in which it has been declared. This renders the whole article valueless as a period piece. So always ensure that what you buy is fully and clearly marked. Faking was often done during the nineteenth century by taking a rather unimportant object such as a small plate, cutting out the hallmark and inserting this with the aid of silver solder into the base of a more important-looking but more modern piece. This act renders the piece value-less except, of course, for the price it would fetch per ounce as scrap silver.

Large silver pieces sometimes bore the initials of their owners and these may have been subsequently removed by grinding and polishing out before sale. It is possible that their removal may have worn away the silver to almost paper thinness. To find out, you should place your hand on one side of the object and run a fingernail gently over the suspect area, watching the other side. If the silver is thin you will easily see the movement of your fingernail under the metal.

During the reign of Queen Victoria it became fashion-able to have a good deal of decoration on silver and, in order to be in the fashion, many owners of early silver sent their pieces to local silversmiths to have decoration added. This was widely done with tea services. Auction catalogues often draw attention to such pieces. A recent item read: 'George II baluster half-pint mug later chased with flowers and scrolls in Victorian times'. This mug would be worth considerably less than if it had been in its original state. In the antique trade, any silver decorated after the original assay date is valued roughly from the date of decoration.

Remember always that silver tarnishes quickly and can become so discoloured that it may look almost like pewter, so do not be put off by appearances. But do beware of repairs. These are often found where handles, feet, lids or spouts join the main body of the article and if the repairs have been done skilfully they may not be easily visible. If you are in doubt, breathe on the suspect part. Soldering will show up as being of a different texture where the condensation from your breath gathers on the surface.

Watch also for wear. This is very common on cutlery. It was often cleaned with an abrasive powder which quickly wore away the bowls of spoons and prongs of forks until the edges became quite sharp. Dents in silver articles, on the other hand, are not so serious: a good silversmith can usually rectify such damage for a relatively small sum.

A final important warning: if you have any doubt as to whether an item, though hallmarked, is silver, a simple test can be made. With the permission of the owner find a part of the object which is not normally visible. Then gently file a portion of the surface with a nail file to remove any dirt or plating. Next, moisten the surface and gently rub the cleaned area with a caustic pencil. If the surface remains clear, then it is fairly certain that the object is silver (or gold). If the object is not silver the moistened area will turn black.

It may sometimes be desirable to take a copy of a hallmark for later study. It is possible to do this by placing a piece of fairly thin paper over the mark and rubbing it with a piece of cobbler's wax (heel ball).

Most fine old silver is very expensive. However, it is still possible to buy representative pieces from most of the Georgian periods which, though small and light in weight, have a charm of their own and at the same time lead to an appreciation of the work of early craftsmen.

Silver has always taken pride of place among collectable items, not because it is any more beautiful than porcelain or glass, nor because it is worth more or less money, but simply because it is so readily standardized in price that buying and selling become less of a gamble. For many years, silver has been bought and sold by its Troy weight and dealers refer to a silver purchase as having cost them so many shillings an ounce. The more beautiful and rare the piece the more shillings per ounce are paid for it. The lowest value is that of scrap silver. This is usually a few shillings under daily prices of silver and is quoted in the Press. It is usually somewhere in the region of 60p per ounce. But weight in itself is a dangerous criterion, so do not think that because someone has paid £8 an ounce for a George III silver teapot-stand weighing six ounces, making a total of £48, you would be safe in paying £160 for one weighing twenty ounces. This stand may contain more silver but the quality of workmanship may be poorer, so you must adjust your price per ounce accordingly, only paying, shall we say, £6 an ounce. On the other hand, a particularly fine and delicate teapot-stand weighing only three ounces may well be worth £10 an ounce. This is possibly one reason why the buying of silver by the ounce is losing favour and more and more people are buying purely on the value of the item's merit. In the end, it is simply a question of deciding how much the article is worth to you.

Most items of silver which fall within the lower price range are either very small or are modern reproductions of older items. Here are some of the less expensive items which may be of interest.

Bonbon dishes

In the Victorian period, these were often delightfully decorated but because they are usually small and light they can still be bought quite cheaply. They look decorative when scattered around a room but are often difficult to clean because of their decoration.

Caddy spoons

These are widely collected and, because of this, usually cost a lot of money for the amount of silver they contain. They allowed the creative imagination of the silversmith to run riot and so appear in the strangest forms and shapes. One of the most sought-after forms is the 'jockey cap', with the peak of the cap forming the spoon handle.

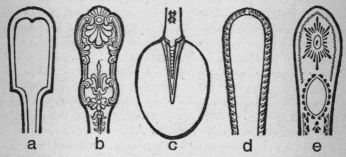

Figure 8 STYLES OF DECORATION ON CUTLERY

(*a*) Fiddle and Thread; (*b*) King's Pattern; (*c*) Rat's Tail; (*d*) Feather Edge; (*e*) Bright Cut

Others were made in the shape of leaves, birds and occasionally fish. There are many Continental caddy spoons, particularly Dutch, and these are usually very much cheaper. But unless you intend to make a collection for display there is little point in buying more than two or three for general use, perhaps in antique tea caddies.

Cutlery

Buying antique silver cutlery can be a very expensive

business. On the other hand, it is a field in which the keen collector can prove himself. With a keen eye and considerable patience, complete sets of cutlery can be assembled over a period of time from odd items for very little money. This is particularly so if you decide to collect a style known as 'fiddle pattern', as for some reason this is at present out of fashion. Other patterns include the King's pattern, reeded edge, rat's tail, feathered, and bright cut. Perhaps the most popular are the bright cut and King's pattern. Sometimes unscrupulous dealers will file away the steps of the fiddle in an attempt to bring spoons into fashion. If you are trying to accumulate a set of matching cutlery, remember to carry a sample with you at all times and do not pay high prices for fish knives and forks. For some reason they are not in great demand and should, therefore, be cheaper.

Knives are always a problem. Few silver-bladed knives exist or, in fact, were ever made. Most good knives of the Georgian and Victorian periods had steel blades with hollow, silver handles. The blades were set into the handles with pitch. These are almost invariably loose and are quite difficult to reset so that they will stand up to the stresses and strains of a solid steak. But steel-bladed knives with bone or ivory handles can be bought quite cheaply. They look well with period silver and are strong, sharp and serviceable. They have one great disadvantage, however; they were made before stainless steel had been invented and rust quickly. The housewife will have to be prepared to clean them regularly with an abrasive.

Sets of coffee, tea, or egg spoons are fairly common, particularly those of the late Georgian or Victorian periods. They are often found in sets of six or twelve, sometimes still in their presentation cases. Apart from their obvious usefulness in the home, they make attractive gifts.

Do not buy spoons or forks which have worn thin at

the tips. They dent and split easily and, as we have pointed out, the edges are often sharp and dangerous. Beware, too, of handles which have been snapped and re-soldered, leaving them weak.

Any cutlery which has pitch-filled handles should never be placed in hot water; to do so will almost certainly loosen them. If they are dented or damaged in any way it is a very costly business to restore them.

Mustard pots

Mustard pots were not always included in cruets and were often made as separate items. Large, decorated-lidded mustard pots with blue glass liners are much sought after and command high prices for their weight. Later smaller and flimsier editions, however, are not so much in demand and can therefore be bought relatively cheaply. Beware of any vessel that has been used for salt and has black spotting on it: this is caused by a chemical action on the silver and is difficult to remove. Blue glass liners should be carefully checked to make sure they fit correctly and can be readily removed. Where they are missing or broken, modern blue glass liners can usually be found or made to replace them.

Napkin rings

These can be found in a great variety of shapes, sizes and designs and do not cost a great deal. Most of them will bear the initials of the original owner engraved in a suitable cartouche. Before buying one, make sure that the silver is thick enough for the initials to be removed if you so wish.

Wine labels

These small labels or tags were suspended by fine chains

from the necks of decanters to identify the contents. They
were very common in late Georgian and Victorian times.
Their shape varies from the straightforward rectangle
(slightly bent or curved to allow it to hug the decanter) to
the very charming leaf-shaped labels decorated with
bunches of grapes and foliage. Although there are collectors of wine labels, quite early Georgian specimens can
still be picked up for a few pounds and they enhance the
appearance of decanters on any sideboard. Smaller labels,
similar in type, were used to identify sauces in cruet
bottles.

It is worth noting that Oriental silver, although slowly
beginning to creep into fashion, is not yet in great
demand and can be bought very reasonably indeed; it is
often as cheap as silver plate.

SHEFFIELD PLATE

In the 1740s, an important discovery was made by a
Sheffield cutler, Thomas Bolsover, which was to have far-
reaching effects on the silver trade. It is said that while he
was repairing the handle of a knife he touched some
copper with heated silver. To his surprise, he found that
the two metals had fused together. He then found that
the metals could be hammered or rolled as though they
were one. He soon realized the possibilities of this discovery; durable articles could now be made that would
look exactly like silver but which would use relatively
little of the precious metal which was, in any case, in very
short supply. Sheffield plate had been born. Bolsover
started by making small articles with the new material –
snuff-boxes, knife handles, thimbles and buttons. Within
a few years, other manufacturers had entered the field.
They were more ambitious and produced tea and coffee

pots, urns, candlesticks and many other articles. The lower cost opened up a large new market. Expensive articles of silver had been symbols of status. The new Sheffield plate was comparatively inexpensive and enjoyed enormous popularity; fine-looking tableware became available to people who could never have afforded to buy real silverware. The industry flourished. By 1762, Sheffield plate was also being made in Birmingham by Matthew Boulton, an enterprising businessman who, in partnership with John Fothergill, founded the Soho Manufactory.

In the early years, the makers of Sheffield plate used their initials to mark their wares. After 1784, the law enabled them to use a symbol or trade mark – a bell, crossed arrows, a pipe, a fish or a ram's head, for example – though there was no legal commitment for makers to do so as there was in the case of silver. In the eighteenth century, many important makers marked their goods with their name and trade mark, but in the early nineteenth century the name was often dropped and the trade mark used alone. Sometimes a crown was used in addition to the maker's mark. This was intended to signify that the piece was of good quality. Nevertheless, much good quality Sheffield plate was completely unmarked.

Sometimes the surface layer of silver on Sheffield plate wears away with cleaning and the red colour of the copper below it shows through; which is one of the ways of identifying Sheffield plate. It was, however, a problem that concerned the makers. In 1830, Samuel Roberts patented a new invention designed to overcome this defect, and within a few years he was using an alloy of copper, nickel and zinc known as German silver (later to be called nickel silver) instead of copper. If the silver layer became worn this 'white alloy' was less obvious than the red copper when exposed.

Within a few years a new discovery led to the final

decline of the Sheffield plate industry. In the 1840s, it was found that a thin layer of silver could be deposited on a base metal 'by electric agency'. So began the manufacture of electro-plate. Electro-plated nickel silver (EPNS) could be produced very cheaply and largely replaced Sheffield plate. These goods can easily be recognized because they are so soft: they are often dented and the thin coating of silver is usually worn by cleaning, leaving dull grey streaks. The only plated ware of real value to the antique collector is Sheffield plate.

BUYING SHEFFIELD PLATE

Do not be too concerned if constant polishing has worn away some of the silver coating from the Sheffield plate you wish to buy. If the wear is slight it does not detract seriously from the value of the piece. If no copper shows, find an edge of the article and pull a fingernail across it. If it is made of Sheffield plate it should be possible to feel a small lip where the silver was hammered over to conceal the edge of the copper. There are several other points to look for which may help with identification and the assessment of value.

Remember that all round objects in Sheffield plate have a seam where the sheet was joined. This runs vertically through the body and is usually found beneath the handle. It may not be obvious but it can be detected by breathing on the surface; the resulting condensation will usually show up the line of the join.

On the more important objects, the manufacturers inserted a solid silver plaque into the side. This was to enable the owners to have their initials engraved without copper showing through. It can be detected by using the condensation test, which will show up the irregular outline of the plaque.

Many articles which were made in silverware were also made in Sheffield plate, though we have never come across any old Sheffield plate cutlery. The work of some eighteenth-century craftsmen is, therefore, still well within the range of the more modest budget.

Sheffield-plated teapots, coffee pots, milk and cream jugs can still be purchased today for less than £25, but if you are buying tea or coffee pots make sure that they are well tinned inside. This tinning was done to prevent the copper from tarnishing and can be recognized by its matt, dark grey appearance. These everyday items can be just as attractive, just as serviceable, and just as antique as some of their silver equivalents.

Wine coasters in Sheffield plate are common. It is obviously desirable to buy them in pairs or in fours, but this is more expensive than buying an odd one and waiting until you find its companions. Designs were repeated many times and the search may well be fruitful. In many cases the green baize will be missing from the base. If so, it is wise to replace it in order to avoid scratching polished surfaces.

Galleried trays (trays which have a wall round the edge) can be bought more cheaply than other types of tray, since the wall considerably limits the number of items that can be placed on them.

THE CARE OF SILVER AND SHEFFIELD PLATE

The most important part of any piece of silver is its hallmark: by this it is dated and identified. Unfortunately, silver tarnishes when exposed to the air and therefore needs frequent cleaning. Unless great care is taken when polishing, a hallmark may be damaged or even removed. Abrasives – even gentle ones such as jewellers' rouge – should be used very sparingly, if at all. The best way to keep silver clean and shining is to wash it regularly in warm, soapy water. The famous silversmith, Paul de Lamerie, sent cleaning instructions with the items he made. 'Clean it now and then with only warm water and soap with a sponge. Then wash it in clean water and dry it well with a soft linen cloth. Keep it in a dry place for damp will spoil it.'

Silver will remain bright for long periods if kept in an airtight display cabinet. If it is being stored for any length of time, it should be wrapped in baize or acid-free tissue paper and removed periodically for washing. Very badly tarnished silver, which has become really black, should be taken to a silversmith for cleaning.

Do not touch silver with the bare fingers more than is absolutely essential, as the small amount of acid on the skin will leave a definite mark on its surface. This applies particularly to silver coins in mint condition. On no account should damaged silver be soldered except by an expert who will use silver solder. Dents in silver should also be removed by an expert. Amateurs who attempt to do so more often than not stretch the metal, making the damage permanent. When cleaning silver candlesticks which are not solid, avoid twisting them round in the duster: this eventually results in the silver itself becoming twisted.

Plate should receive exactly the same care and treatment as silver. Constant use of abrasives will remove the thin surface layer and expose the baser metal beneath.

CHAPTER FIVE

NON-PRECIOUS METALS

Brass and Copper

IN general, brass and copper have never achieved a high value in the antique trade, with a few notable exceptions. Very old brass and copper pieces of the four-teenth, fifteenth and sixteenth centuries are worth sub-stantial sums because of their rarity but, on the whole, brass and copper articles from the eighteenth century onwards are worth comparatively little. Yet people who collect these metals value them highly and tend to dis-believe those in the trade who regard their treasures as little more than interesting collections of curios. Many copper and brass articles end up in country inns and cot-tages. They seem to need a homely setting and go well with dark oak beams.

The vogue for collecting old horse brasses created a certain demand for these but the flood of mass-produced modern copies and the never-ending task of cleaning has tended to push them out of favour again. Nevertheless, some people are still keen and it is worth noting some of the characteristics of old horse brasses. Remember that a genuine antique brass was fitted to the horse's harness and should show signs of wear on the underside, a smooth polish resulting from constant movement against the leather strap on which it hung. This should be par-ticularly obvious on the buckle-shaped loop by which it was attached. These old brasses usually had two small studs on the underside by which the brass was held in a vice when it was cut by the craftsmen. Occasionally they bear a date. The best period for horse brasses was between about 1800 and 1875. After that they were stamped out by machine. Modern reproductions which have been moulded are usually rough and have a narrower hanging-loop.

There is still a certain demand for old brass candle-sticks, and old copper and brass cooking utensils are still bought, sometimes for use but more often for home decoration. Old copper jelly moulds of the Victorian period and copper coal scuttles, particularly those of helmet shape, sell well. Some early pierced brass fireside equipment is well worth looking for, since it was designed by great furniture designers such as Hepplewhite and Sheraton and is most attractive. The old fire rests make good door stops, and old brass trivets are often very useful in the modern hearth. There is even a demand among interior decorators for old brass bedsteads which, a few years ago, could be seen on rubbish dumps or blocking gaps in farm hedges.

Brass candlesticks are today cast in the same shapes and forms as they were during the eighteenth century. The only discernible difference in many cases are the brazing marks. Early candlesticks of the period around 1700 were made in two halves which were then brazed together leaving the stem hollow, a useful saving of metal. The foot, which was cast separately, was then brazed to the stem. Old candlesticks have had their edges and mouldings softened by years of cleaning.

Very few great craftsmen worked in either copper or brass. It is worth remembering that late Victorian brass often shows a registration mark which makes it possible to decide the year in which the particular design was introduced.

Bronze

Unlike copper and brass, bronze has always been a popular material with artists and craftsmen. The price of objects of quality in this metal is high. Because of its serviceability and its lasting finish, bronze was often used for works of art which were to be exposed to the elements. The Italians used it a great deal for statuary and for crucibles, mortars and pestles and they often partially gilded it. It was widely used for cast decoration, clocks, candlesticks, candelabra, etc., and during the eighteenth century became *the* metal in which artists cast their sculptures. It was also very popular during the French Regency period. A good deal of spelter masquerades as bronze: it is worthless, although it sometimes fetches unreasonable sums in London antique markets which are so affected by the whims and fashions of the interior decorators.

Iron

This has never been a popular metal for artistic work for the obvious reason that it rusts very quickly and therefore does not last well, though iron jewellery has been made and it is rare and fetches high prices. Iron has been used extensively for kitchen implements and for fire grates and andirons. Firebacks, large metal plates which stood behind the fire basket in large open grates, were usually in decorated cast iron. Early specimens, some of which include a date in the decoration, can still be found.

Lead

This was a popular metal during the eighteenth century for garden ornaments, figures, fountains and suchlike. Water tanks and flower boxes were also made of lead. All these are very much sought after and are collectors' pieces; though, once again, nineteenth-century and present day copyists have tended to detract from their value. Smaller items, such as tobacco boxes, can be bought quite reasonably. Many late examples were made from ammunition melted down after the Crimean War.

Pewter

Pewter is usually an alloy of tin and lead – and was used for centuries as the poor man's silver, particularly for household utensils.

There were three standards which might be described as hard, medium and soft – technically known as hard, trifle and lay. When pewter articles were first made they were highly polished and looked rather like a dull silver, but as soon as the air got to them oxidization took place and they took on the familiar grey pewter colour. Except for the oldest and rarest pieces, pewter is still quite cheap to buy, since its rather drab appearance makes it unsuitable for elegant settings.

The age of pewter can be judged by its patina, that is to say the depth and hardness of the surface oxidization; by the shape and style of the manufacture; and by the touchmarks which are rather similar to the hallmarks on silver. These touchmarks were stamped into the article by the maker and each was registered with the Pewterers' Company on a touch plate. One of the commonest touchmarks is that of the Tudor rose surmounted by a crown. This was a mark of standard quality. Pieces of superior quality carry an 'X' mark. There are often initials of the maker and there is sometimes a date. Many pieces of pewter were illegally stamped with silver hallmarks with intent to deceive.

In 1824, it became obligatory to stamp all drinking vessels with their capacity, together with the initials of the reigning monarch. Tankards made since 1824 should, therefore, bear the initials G.R., W.R., or V.R., depending on whether they were made during the reign of George IV, William IV, or Queen Victoria. From 1877, a crown was added to the V.R. and this is an easy way to recognize a late piece.

Pewter made during the seventeenth century is rare because, as pieces became worn or were damaged, they were melted down and re-made.

Pewter is a very malleable metal. Treat it carefully: once dented it becomes stretched, making it difficult, if not impossible, to knock out the dent without leaving a mark. Great care should be used when cleaning all types of pewter. The touchmark (see Illus. 12) corresponds to the hallmark on silver, and if this is worn away both the interest and value of the piece are reduced. Whether or not pewter should be cleaned is largely a matter of taste: some people like to see it dull, others like it highly polished to look almost like silver. But pewter does not polish easily and to burnish it with any sort of abrasive will destroy its value. There are several proprietary cleaners on the market which can be used safely: but in general it is true to say that old pewter should not be cleaned.

Tinware

Tableware made of tin was fairly common from the sixteenth century until the middle of the nineteenth century, but its metallic finish gives it little attraction. However, japanning, widely used in the eighteenth and early nineteenth century in imitation of Oriental lacquer work, was used on some tinware. Colour varnishes were applied to the metal, which was then baked to produce a hard glossy finish. All kinds of utensils were treated in this way – coffee pots, water cans, tea canisters and buckets. The bargees on English canals always favoured painted tinware. The background is usually dark – black, brown, olive-green or deep crimson – and the decoration usually consists of sprays of flowers, festoons of leaves or birds with gay plumage. In the 1830s, painted tin trays were common. One of the most famous factories producing this ware was at Pontypool.

Britannia Metal

'White metal', as it was called at the end of the eighteenth century, or 'Britannia metal' to give it the later and more familiar name, is an alloy consisting largely of tin with some antimony and a small addition of copper. The metal was cheap and between about 1805 and 1830 captured the pewter market. It was harder, brighter and less liable to crack than pewter, but was nevertheless malleable and fairly easily worked. The chief producer at this time was the Sheffield firm of Dixon and his work is usually marked. At a later date Britannia metal was often electro-plated with silver.

Britannia metal is regarded as the curse of the antique dealer's life. In the words of John Bright: 'Silence is golden; speech is silvern. But to say one thing and mean another is Britannia metal.' Thousands of items were made from it – teapots with sugar basins and cream jugs, coffee pots, boxes, etc – and so far it has been of little value, though there are now rumours of a developing American market. Unfortunately, many tea-sets and gilded clocks made from this base metal are sold for quite large sums to unsuspecting buyers who, if they ever try to sell, will find extreme difficulty in getting any offers at all. Remember that when in good condition an item made of Britannia metal can look magnificent. So, never buy without testing. If filed, the file will bite deeply into the metal under very little pressure. Britannia metal and other similar alloys are often referred to in the trade as 'spelter'.

CHAPTER SIX

PORCELAIN

PORCELAIN is one of the most rewarding fields for the collector of antiques; so many of the pieces have great beauty. Many experts say that the making of high-quality porcelain began and ended in China. It was certainly being made there when William the Conqueror invaded Britain and by the middle of the seventeenth century Chinese porcelain was being imported in fair quantity when the East India Trading Company was bringing in tea. But we did not make any porcelain in this country until the middle of the eighteenth century. It is generally agreed that the first factories to produce English porcelain were at Bow and Chelsea in London, at Longton Hall in Staffordshire, and Lund's Factory in Bristol. They all started commercial manufacture between 1745 and 1750, using a soft-paste body. In 1768 William Cookworthy, a Plymouth chemist who had been experimenting for some years with local materials, founded the first English factory to make a type of hard-paste porcelain, although several Continental makers had already discovered the secret – the Meissen factory near Dresden, for one. Hard paste was an improvement on the soft paste of the early factories since it made it possible to reproduce on a hard-textured surface the high glazes which were so much admired in the imported Chinese porcelain. William Cookworthy's secret was later taken to Bristol and eventually to a factory at New Hall in Staffordshire.

Great emphasis is laid by many experts on the ability to distinguish between hard-paste and soft-paste porcelain and it is certainly useful to be able to do so because to identify a piece as made of soft paste places it as an early piece – as eighteenth century. However, this ability comes only with experience and the amateur need not worry overmuch if it does not come easily.

Much of the porcelain produced by the early factories was decorated in the blue designs derived from those that had become familiar on the imported Chinese ware. This decoration is often referred to as 'in the Chinese taste'. Although this early blue and white porcelain is widely collected, it can still be bought for comparatively small sums compared with later items decorated with coloured enamels.

Of all types of porcelain the figures, particularly if they can be found in pairs or sets, are probably the most desirable. Many of these figures were copied from Continental designs, though personalities of the day such as actors and actresses were also popular.

It will probably be useful here to make brief reference to the history of the best-known English factories making porcelain.

Chelsea

We know that this factory was making porcelain in 1745 as marked specimens exist with 'Chelsea 1745' under the glaze. George II interested himself in its output and encouraged German and other foreign workmen to come to work there. Indeed, the first name associated with the factory came from Belgium – Nicholas Sprimont – and most of the best work at Chelsea was done under his direction in the early years. But by then it had already been decided that the factory must be sold and Sprimont's influence declined. In 1770, it was bought by William Duesbury of the Derby factory, who carried on the Chelsea production for fourteen years. This is known as the Chelsea-Derby period and the work shows considerable French influence. It is thought that for much of the time the Chelsea factory was used as a centre for the decoration of porcelain made in Derby.

Bow

This factory was run by an Irishman, Thomas Frye, who took out patents for his methods of making porcelain 'not inferior in beauty and fineness' to the porcelain of China and Japan. He managed it from 1745 until 1759 but relatively few pieces are known which were made before 1750. Many figures were made, some of them in imitation of Meissen figures, others original. Some of these had a hole at the back into which a candle-holder could be placed. The factory closed between 1775 and 1778 (the actual date is uncertain) and it is probable that Duesbury of Derby took over the stock and equipment.

Derby

Porcelain was probably made at Derby as early as 1745 but early Derby porcelain, as we know it, is associated with the name of William Duesbury. Before he operated his Derby factory in 1756 he had controlled a workshop in London, decorating white porcelain mainly from Bow and Chelsea. Much of the early Derby work shows the influence of Chelsea but after the acquisition of the Chelsea factory in 1770 the style changed.

Duesbury employed first-class artists as modellers and decorators, as did his son who took over the factory after his death in 1786. Among them were John Bacon, William Coffee and Pierre Stephen. The painting in the years between 1770 and 1795 is often superbly done. The decorators specialized: landscapes were done by Boreman (who had learned his craft at Chelsea) and Hill; birds and fruit by Complin; flowers by Pegg and Billingsley; while Bamford specialized in the classical styles.

After 1795, there were many changes and other artists began to take over – John and Robert Brewer (landscapes), Dodson (birds) and Steele (fruit) were among them. But quality was beginning to decline a little, a decline which accelerated when Robert Bloor rented the factory from 1815. Even so, standards were still high when compared with the work of nineteenth-century porcelain makers. Bloor died in 1845 and the factory closed down in 1848. The present Royal Crown Derby Porcelain Company started in 1876.

Longton Hall

This factory was producing soft-paste porcelain in Staffordshire for some ten years from about 1750 to 1760. It is noted for moulded porcelain in the form of leaves on dinner ware, and for its figures. Longton Hall is thought to have pioneered the use of cobalt blue as a colouring.

Lund's (Bristol) and Worcester

A factory in Bristol known as Lund's was certainly making soft-paste porcelain in 1750, probably earlier, but by 1752 it had moved with a number of its workers to Worcester. The name usually associated with this move is that of Dr John Wall, though he was only one partner and did not assume the major direction of the factory until four years before he died in 1776.

Nevertheless, this early period from 1752 until the factory was sold to Thomas Flight in 1783 (seven years after Wall's death) is usually known as the 'Dr Wall period'. One of the chief decorators was Robert Hancock, who came from the Battersea factory in 1756 and worked in Worcester until 1774. In 1793, Martin Barr became a

partner and the names of Flight and Barr were linked
with the factory until 1840.

When Flight took over after the 'Dr Wall period', one
of the decorators in the factory, Robert Chamberlain, established with his brother a second factory in Worcester
which continued for many years and was so successful
that it took over the Flight and Barr Company and the
two continued as a single enterprise.

Meanwhile, in 1812, another porcelain factory was established in Worcester by Thomas Grainger, who was related to Chamberlain, but its work was not of particularly
high quality. This factory was also taken over at a later
date by the firm founded by Chamberlain which, in 1862,
became the Worcester Royal Porcelain Factory.

Plymouth, Bristol and New Hall

When William Cookworthy of Plymouth was experimenting with hard-paste porcelain he had links with
Richard Champion in Bristol, who fired some of his ex-
perimental pieces for him. It was not until 1768 that
Cookworthy set up a factory of his own. Despite the fact
that some excellent work was produced, it was not a commercial success – perhaps because there was too high a
proportion of imperfect pieces. He moved his factory to
Bristol when he was already a man of sixty-five. Within
two years he had retired and Champion took over the
manufacture of the new hard-paste porcelain, improving
the technical quality. A number of well-known artists
worked in Bristol, including Henry Bone who later
became a Royal Academician.

Legal expenses involved in the protection of the hard-
paste patent rights against attacks by Staffordshire
interests led by Josiah Wedgwood were too much for
Champion's resources. He was forced to sell to a company
which started a factory at New Hall in Staffordshire. He

also agreed to give advice and help. It specialized in ware decorated 'in the Chinese taste', much of it for export to the Continent.

Lowestoft

This factory, which was founded in 1757, produced porcelain similar in many ways to the Bow products and it seems more than probable that it had secured the services of someone who had acquired his 'know-how' from Bow. Much tableware was produced, decorated in blue 'in the Chinese taste' or, sometimes in later pieces, in a characteristic shade of pink.

Caughley

This Shropshire factory, which had been making earthenware for some twenty years previously, was acquired in 1772 by Thomas Turner (who had previously been at the Worcester factory) and started making porcelain. Caughley, like Worcester, used transfer printing as a means of decoration and Robert Hancock was responsible for many of the engravings. The factory was the first to use the 'willow pattern' design which appeared in 1780, later to become so popular on both porcelain and pottery. In 1799, John Rose, who had worked at Caughley and had later established a pottery of his own, bought the Caughley factory. Its porcelain is very similar to that of Worcester. When unmarked, identification is usually based on decoration, the subject and the colouring.

Coalport

This was a second factory, often known as.Coalbrookdale, set up by John Rose, in which much Caughley porcelain was decorated. In 1814, the Caughley factory was closed and the equipment and workers moved to Coalport. Later, Rose acquired the moulds from the South Wales factories at Nantgarw and Swansea. Today the Coalport China Company operates at Stoke-on-Trent.

Nantgarw and Swansea

The name of William Billingsley is closely linked with Nantgarw, a small village north of Cardiff. Billingsley was a rolling-stone. He had started as an apprentice in the Derby factory and worked there as a flower painter. He then spent five years at a small factory he had started near Mansfield (at Pinxton) where he made porcelain. (Specimens are now rare and expensive.) Billingsley then became a freelance decorator, went to Worcester for several years and then started making porcelain again at Nantgarw. Here, and at the Swansea works of Lewis Dillwyn between 1813 and 1819, some superb porcelain was made. Much of it was decorated in London and connoisseurs value it as highly as some of the finest French porcelain. But Billingsley had his financial troubles. He moved on again to work for John Rose at Coalport and by 1823 the manufacture of porcelain at Nantgarw and Swansea had ceased.

Later English Factories

By the early nineteenth century, four other factories were also making porcelain – Davenport, Spode and Minton in Staffordshire and Rockingham in Yorkshire. It was sometimes rather ornate and overdecorated but was extremely well made. At the Davenport factory, much Derby work was copied and decorators from the Derby factory were employed there.

The Spode factory specialized in tableware, adding to the prosperity of a thriving earthenware business, and is usually credited with having evolved bone china. It later became the Copeland factory.

Much of Minton's earlier output was decorated with Japanese designs and, later, Derby-style motifs with fruit and flowers were used.

At Rockingham, which only started to make porcelain about 1820, tablewares, especially in blue and green, were produced in quantity. Most of the output was gilded. Rockingham porcelain is now sought keenly by collectors, especially pieces with the celebrated 'griffin' mark.

The porcelain made at the Belleek factory in County Fermanagh, Ireland, gained a considerable reputation in the second half of the nineteenth century. Using a French process, the hard porcelain was glazed so that it gained a nacreous lustre (like mother-of-pearl). It could be worked into the thinnest of layers without losing its strength and this made it possible to model the most delicate baskets decorated mainly with small leaves of shamrock and tiny flowers such as lily of the valley. These usually had a handle like woven cane and sometimes a cover. The work was done by hand and it is sometimes possible to see faintly the fingerprints of the modellers on the petals of the flowers. These baskets often carry the name of the factory on a ribbon of porcelain fixed to the base. Most of this work was done between about 1860 and 1880 when the owner was a wealthy man who could pay first-class artists and craftsmen without being overconcerned about his profit. The Belleek factory also produced parian statuary, plant pot holders, and ordinary tableware.

BUYING PORCELAIN

Although much porcelain is marked, the only true safeguard when buying fine pieces is to be able to recognize the characteristics of products from the more important factories. Given this skill, the reader may at some time be fortunate enough to recognize a rare piece where he least expects to find it, perhaps in a shop where the owner may have dismissed it as unimportant. It is discoveries of this kind that make the whole business of antique collecting so exciting.

Chelsea

Much early Chelsea ware shows small, crescent-shaped bubbles in the paste when held against a strong light. These are known as 'Chelsea moons' and are distinctive of this factory. The glaze has a soft, 'cheesey' appearance.

Bow

This factory produced a ware that was extremely heavy for its size and the glaze on the so-called 'white ware' looks like a thick coating of condensed milk. Many of the figures have quite large firing cracks (Illus. 21).

Chelsea-Derby

Many eighteenth-century Derby and Chelsea figures have three distinct 'patch' marks under the base rather resembling thumb prints (see Illus. 22). These were made by the pads on which the figures stood when they were fired in the kiln.

Worcester

Early Worcester porcelain when held to a strong light shows a distinct greenish tinge in the paste. A pencil drawn around the inside ring of a foot rim will usually mark the porcelain in places where the glaze has shrunk, exposing the biscuit surface (Illus. 20).

Caughley

Although superficially rather similar in appearance to
early Worcester, Caughley porcelain shows a yellow or
brownish tinge when held against a strong light.

Plymouth

Porcelain from the Plymouth factory is heavy for its size
and often has small, black imperfections on the surface. It
is particularly noted for its salt cellars and sweetmeat or
pickle stands, which were made in the form of scallop
shells.

For most people, early porcelain from the famous factories will be too expensive, but much attractive porcelain
was made in the nineteenth century when mass production first came in and decoration was applied by transfer. The potters took advantage of new techniques and,
because of this, there was less opportunity for expressing
artistic flair. Colours, although much improved in their
technical application, lost much of their vigour and
figures particularly lost charm and spontaneity. This does
not mean, however, that nineteenth-century porcelain is
not worth collecting, for much of it, though not as beautiful as that produced by the craftsmen of the earlier
famous factories, has a charm characteristic of the period,
and often looks well in modern settings. It is still possible
to buy quite important pieces from the Coalport, Davenport, Minton, Rockingham and Spode factories for less
than £20 and they are nearly always clearly marked and
are, as yet, not important enough for the forger to copy.
Variations in style and decoration are limitless and nearly
everything that could possibly be required – from vases to
dinner services – is still plentiful. Beware, however, of
vulgar decoration, brash, brightly applied gilding, garish

colour combinations, and thoughtless design. Nineteenth-century porcelain is superior to earlier work in one respect. Technical advances greatly improved glazes and their application: they became clearer and smoother and were rarely damaged in the firing process.

It is worth noting that French biscuit porcelain is still very plentiful. This is usually seen in the form of figures produced by firing in an unglazed state so that the surface is left rough to the touch. They were coloured with rather anaemic shades, often highlighted with gilding, and are seldom marked, apart from a number of scratches made in the base before firing, though the telltale crossed '7' sometimes confirms their Continental origin.

Marks can be of great value in the identification of porcelain and pottery, and are discussed fully in the next chapter.

THE CARE OF PORCELAIN

Water used for washing decorated porcelain should never contain strong detergents as these might damage the enamels. Delicately-made pieces of porcelain should never be dried with a cloth, as it is difficult to judge how much pressure can safely be applied to the fragile parts – the fingers on a figure, for example. Instead, allow the piece to drain and dry at room temperature after rinsing it in clean water. The best way to clean intricate decorated work, such as Belleek baskets of flowers, is to keep the piece constantly on the move in the washing water, removing it occasionally to blow into crevices where dust may have collected. It is always dangerous to use a small brush as even a single bristle may stick and be enough to break some of the finer and thinner parts.

Fine hair-cracks in plain undecorated porcelain can be

made less obvious by careful application of a diluted bleaching liquid.

It is still all too common to find antique plates which have been used in an oven. This results in a network of small cracks in the glaze known as 'crazing'. It is very pleasant to use antique china when possible, but always avoid overheating of this kind.

For many years damaged porcelain was regarded as worthless and was difficult to sell. In recent years the position has changed. There are now signs that some collectors are prepared to accept slight damage if the piece is rare enough or until they find a perfect piece to replace it. If the damage completely ruins the appearance of a piece, there are some very good porcelain restorers who will repair it so well that few people will spot the repair without the aid of ultra-violet radiation. Such repairs, however, cost a good deal of money and estimates should always be asked for before the work is commissioned. The names and addresses of porcelain restorers can be found in the *British Antiques Year Book*.

CHAPTER SEVEN

POTTERY

IN dealing with porcelain, we have described briefly the various factories where it was made. Earthenware or pottery has been made without a break since pre-historic times and many more factories have been involved since it began to be made on a commercial scale. We shall, therefore, approach the subject from a technical point of view, dealing with the various types of pottery and the development of techniques in the use of raw materials and decorative media.

Pottery is distinguished from porcelain by holding the object against a strong light. Porcelain will normally allow a certain amount of light to pass through it; pottery is always opaque. There are, however, certain articles made of heavy, thick porcelain which are also opaque. Pottery is literally the poor man's porcelain. Popular porcelain items of a period were often copied in pottery: they were cheaper to make because the raw materials consisted of simple clays which can be found in abundance in Britain, whereas porcelain required the careful mixing of many ingredients. The clays for porcelain were more difficult to obtain and the firing at higher temperatures was more hazardous.

Most pottery can be bought quite cheaply, except for some very early specimens and the very fine Wedgwood wares. Some of the best-known types are here described.

Slipware

Potters in the seventeenth and eighteenth centuries often worked in a small town or village producing articles for the home – dishes, pots, mugs, etc. These were made from local clays and were decorated with slip – a white or coloured clay in a thick creamy condition which was 'slipped' across the surface of the article like decorative icing on a cake. Sometimes several different coloured slips were used, and these were trailed across the article from a spouted vessel or quill, or dropped or dotted on with a brush. Powdered lead ore was then dusted over the article before firing.

The earliest dated slipware was made at Wrotham in Kent and in London in the seventeenth century, and signed dishes with pictorial designs were made in Staffordshire by Thomas Toft in the reign of Charles II. Fine slipware was also made in Derbyshire in the eighteenth century.

The making of slipware has continued until the present day and it is not easy to date a piece. Only the real expert can decide on the age and origin of certain pieces. Early slipware is much sought after by collectors but may be overlooked by antique dealers who regard the crude brown, yellow and red decoration as undistinguished. A jug made by Ralph Simpson of Burslem decorated with a tulip design in brown, signed and dated 1691, recently sold for £1,700.

English Delft

The pottery known as 'Delft' is made by a process which has been used in many parts of the world for centuries; it was certainly perfected by the Italian potters as early as the fifteenth century for making majolica. Clay is used to make a plate or vessel and is then fired. The resulting article, which is porous like a modern flowerpot, is then dipped in an opaque white glaze containing an oxide of tin. On this white surface the decorators painted their designs, usually in cobalt blue. Over this, a transparent glaze was usually applied and the article was then fired a second time. Delft as we know it was first made in Holland from the sixteenth century and took its name from the town of Delft. By the middle of the seventeenth century it was being made in England; Lambeth, Bristol and Liverpool were the main centres (English delft is usually spelt with a small 'd').

Portraits of royalty were a popular form of decoration and so were flowers, legendary scenes and landscapes showing Chinese influence. Perhaps the commonest examples of delft are found in tiles which were made for use in fireplaces and kitchens. These often portrayed biblical scenes and some were decorated in such a way that it took several tiles to complete a picture.

The largest output of delft was probably from Lambeth, where there are said to have been as many as twenty potteries. The white glaze was thin and some Lambeth delft has a slight reddish tinge where the body shows through. The blue used in decoration has a grey tone.

Bristol delft is noted for its polychrome decoration (ie, using more than one colour), particularly for delicate shades of purple and green. Some pieces have a type of decoration known as *bianco sopra bianco*, in which white is painted over the enamel (often purple) to give a lace-like finish. It is seen particularly on the borders of plates. Most Bristol delft has a greenish tinge in the glaze.

Liverpool delft has a bluish tinge in the glaze. The punch bowls made in Liverpool are famous and the factory of Sadler & Green started transfer printing on delftware, a process which was to revolutionize the methods of pottery decoration in later years.

Salt-glazed Stonewares

Stoneware was made from a good plastic clay mixed with sand or some other form of silica. The shaped articles were placed in perforated boxes or saggers made from waste scraps. This was to protect the ware when it was fired at a high temperature in the kiln. With most clays the resulting colour was brown, ranging from a light buff colour to a dark sepia. The stoneware was glazed by throwing salt into the kiln when the heat was intense.

A grey salt-glazed stoneware was extensively made in Germany and Holland more than 300 years ago. By the end of the seventeenth century several potters were producing stoneware in England – John Dwight in Fulham, James Morley in Nottingham and John and David Elers, who started in London and later moved to Staffordshire. 'There were, about the year 1700, twenty-two glazing ovens in Burslem, each with eight mouths; and around each of them was a scaffold, on which men stood to throw salt into the ovens. The salt was decomposed by the heat of the oven; and holes in the saggers allowed the fumes to enter and act upon the wares within the saggers.' Shortly after this, new stoneware factories started in Derbyshire, notably at Chesterfield, using local clays.

Developments in Staffordshire

John and David Elers were Dutch and had had some experience as silversmiths. Much of their work had great artistic merit. They discovered a fine-grained, iron-stained clay at Bradwell Wood in Staffordshire which produced a red stoneware and their unglazed teapots of this material were beautifully made with decoration moulded in relief. It is said that the brothers were very jealous of their manufacturing secrets and looked to strategy rather than to the law for protection, keeping a careful guard against strangers and employing labour with little intelligence. However, their methods became known to Twyford and Astbury, according to some earlier writers, by stealth.

Twyford applied for employment at the works, and proceeded to manifest entire carelessness and indifference to all the operations going on. Astbury was more of a hero; he suffered bodily in the cause. He assumed the garb and appearance of an idiot, got into employ, and submitted to the cuffs, kicks and unkind treatment of masters and men with meekness. He ate his food and went through the easy drudgery of his employment and comported himself in all outward matters with the same apparent imbecility. But his eyes and his mind were wide awake all the time. He watched every process by stealth; and on returning home in the evenings, he constructed models of all the different apparatus he had seen during the day, and made memoranda of the processes. This course he continued for two years; at the expiration of which period his employers began to think that he was not quite the fool they had imagined and he was discharged.

That is the story and there is no doubt that Twyford and Astbury had started to make ware similar to the Elers' products by about 1710, and other factories followed. Astbury later developed a white, salt-glazed ware by adding calcined flint to the clay. There is also a colourful story to account for this discovery.

Mr Astbury, being on a journey to London, had arrived at Dunstable, when he was compelled to seek a remedy for the eyes of his horse, which seemed to be rapidly going blind. The hostler of the tavern at which he stayed burned a flint stone till quite red; then he pulverized it very fine, and by blowing a little of the dust into each eye, occasioned both to discharge much matter, and be quite benefited. Mr Astbury having noticed the white colour of the calcined flint, the ease with which it was then reduced to powder, and its clayey nature when discharged in the moisture from the horse's eye, immediately conjectured that it might be usefully employed to render of a different colour the pottery he made.

Whatever the source of his inspiration, and it seems more likely that it came from earlier potters such as John Dwight or from the glassmakers who were already using calcined flint, the white-glazed stoneware (though it was, in fact, cream in colour) was certainly being made commercially by about 1720, and was widely used later by Aaron Woods and the two Ralph Woods, by Enoch Wood and by the Thomas Whieldon-Josiah Wedgwood partnership (Wedgwood was then in his twenties).

It is worth mentioning here that Wedgwood later made large quantities of a black, unglazed stoneware by adding manganese oxide to the mixture to be fired. It had a hard fine texture and was known as 'black basalts' (after the hard, dark, volcanic, basalt rock). For this he established a factory at Shelton, which developed later into his main Etruria Works. All kinds of tableware were made in black basalt, together with decorative statues and vases which depended for their appeal entirely on form and character. The clay was pressed into moulds giving a decoration in bas relief, usually with classical motifs. By the early nineteenth century many Staffordshire firms were making black basalt.

A development which followed the manufacture of white salt-glazed ware and involved greater concentration on decoration and colouring is associated with the name of Thomas Whieldon. Moulded flowers and leaves were placed as relief decoration on the main body and were joined by thin rolls of clay to provide the stems. He also perfected new colouring techniques, using a liquid lead glaze which could be dabbed with metallic oxides of various colours before firing, producing marbling, mottling, and tortoiseshell effects. Whieldon also produced agate ware, which was made by mixing layers of various shades of coloured clay together into a single mass before working. This gave the ware a streaked or variegated appearance (see Illus. 25). Whieldon agate ware is usually rather thin and light.

Josiah Wedgwood had fifteen years' experience in the pottery industry, first as an apprentice and later as a partner with Whieldon, before starting a business of his own. He set himself to improve the stoneware on which he had worked with Whieldon in an attempt to produce an earthenware body which would have some of the properties of porcelain. He first succeeded in producing a cream ware which was hard, attractive in appearance, and had a soft rich glaze. It is also extremely light in the hand. Wedgwood made a cream-ware tea-set as a gift for Queen Charlotte who allowed him to call this new earthenware 'Queen's ware'. This was in 1765; he had to wait another ten years before he could make a further improvement, though he had already solved the technical problems. Litigation was involved, since William Cookworthy had patented the use of Cornish clay and stone. However, by 1775, Wedgwood was able to add these ingredients to his raw materials. By 1779, he was producing 'pearl ware' which was whiter than his cream ware and lent itself to transfer decoration (see p 82). This was to lead to a great expansion in the pottery industry and a considerable export trade. Other potteries were soon producing similar wares, notably a Yorkshire pottery at Leeds.

Among Wedgwood's best-known achievements was the manufacture of his jasper ware, a fine, hard stoneware in

which the body consisted largely of sulphate of barytes
with only about forty per cent of clay. It has fine texture
and a smooth, almost wax-like surface, like some porcelain. When it was introduced in 1775 it was coloured
throughout, since the colour had been mixed with the
body. Slowly, the solid jasper was replaced by what is
known as jasper dip, in which the colour was applied to
the white body. Blue is the commonest colour of jasper
ware, but it was also made in black and shades of green,
pink and lilac.

Apart from tableware and decorative vases, jasper ware
was used to make snuff boxes, scent bottles, plaques for
interior decoration and even ear-rings, cameos and
buttons, the designs standing out in relief – white figures,
medallions and classical motifs against a smooth,
coloured groundwork.

The Wedgwood firm employed many famous modellers and designers at Etruria, including artists from
Italy. This was due to the influence of Wedgwood's partner, Thomas Bentley, a wealthy Liverpool merchant who
was a student of the fine arts.

We have referred several times in previous pages to
transfer printing which, in the first half of the nineteenth
century, was used by almost every pottery in the country.
Here is a contemporary account of the process.

In that very useful production, the *blue-printed*
ware, the pattern is engraved upon a copper plate; the
ink or blue paint is a viscid mixture of cobalt, flint, oil,
tar and other substances; and a print is taken from the
plate with this ink on a piece of very thin but tough
paper. The paper is handed to a girl called the *cutter*,
who cuts away from it as much of the unprinted part as
is not wanted; and a woman, called the *transferrer*,
places the paper with the inked side downwards, on the
biscuit ware which is to receive the pattern. She rubs

the paper with a roll of flannel in such a way as to transfer the ink from the paper to the biscuit ware; and by washing the ware immediately afterwards in water, all the paper is washed off in fragments, leaving the inked pattern on the ware ... The ink has a dirty brown appearance when laid on, but the heat of an oven and the subsequent glazing bring out its lively blue tint.

Vast quantities of this blue and white transfer ware were made, particularly large dinner services, and there was a considerable export to America.

The better-class transfer-printed ware was sold to middle-class people who could not afford to buy porcelain, the rougher pieces went to the homes of the workers. Certain patterns were widely used – the willow pattern 'in the Chinese taste', a design known as 'Asiatic pheasant' with flowers and birds, and the 'wild rose' pattern, which depicted a country scene with a river, a bridge, boatmen and some distant houses. The latter took its name from its floral border. Among famous makers of this type of decoration ware were W. Adams & Son, J. & R. Clews, A. Stevenson, and the Spode factory, which produced work of very fine quality.

Most transfer-printed earthenware was produced in the first half of the nineteenth century and, on the whole, the earlier work tends to be the better.

A summary of the main developments in the making and decoration of earthenware must include some reference to lustre ware. Its production involved coating the whole or part of the surface of glazed earthenware articles with a metallic oxide to produce a gold, silver or copper sheen. Its use was often combined with colour decoration. Lustre was certainly made before 1800 but the finer types came a little later, between 1810 and 1830. These are known as 'resist' lustres. Before coating with lustre, the desired design was painted on the article with fine china clay mixed with a sticky or resinous medium – glycerine, for example. This resisted the coating of metallic oxide which could be removed, so that the design was left against a lustred background.

Nearly every earthenware factory made lustre of some kind. Some specialized in a particular type, though few bear the maker's mark. At Newcastle and Sunderland, lustre was combined with transfer printing.

BUYING POTTERY

When an expert handles a piece of porcelain or pottery he almost invariably looks first at the base or the back to see whether it is marked in any way. The mark or marks give him some guidance about the maker and the date, but he will treat marks with caution, especially in the case of porcelain, since many early marks have been copied or faked. Marks may have been impressed into the soft clay body before firing, much as a footprint is made in soft damp sand, or printed or painted in colour on the biscuit before glazing. These are 'underglaze' marks. Other marks have been painted on top of the glaze and these are obviously easier to fake at a later date. Factory marks can provide much useful information. The amateur will find it useful to remember the following facts when examining the marks on porcelain or pottery: they help to narrow the field for further investigation.

1. If the words 'England' or 'Made in England' are found, the article is not an antique. The former was used after 1891 (though a few firms used it from about 1880); the latter appears from about 1900 and is still used today. It became necessary to use the 'England' mark on ceramics because the Americans insisted that all imported

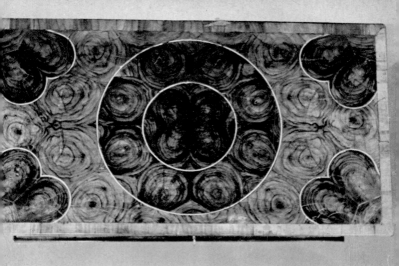

1. Oyster-shell veneering on a William and Mary chest

2. Sunburst inlay commonly used in the reign of George I

3. Marquetry work on a nineteenth-century French desk

4. Dowelling on early oak furniture

5. Split-pin used to secure a drawer handle

6. Dovetailing on the drawer of a Queen Anne chest

7. Cross-banding on the edge of a Queen Anne chest

8. Interior of an early Georgian drawer showing the grain of the base board running from front to back

9. Interior of a drawer in a Sheraton washstand and dressing table

10. The corner of a Queen Anne dressing mirror. The walnut veneer has been applied in sections; note the gesso edge and the marking on the mirror plate

11. A typical Georgian silver hallmark. *From left to right:* Maker's mark; Lion Passant; Date Letter (1741-2); Leopard's Head Crowned

12. A touchmark on late eighteenth-century London pewter

13. Acanthus leaf decoration on a Georgian silver sauce tureen

14. Classical decoration around the base of a George III butter dish

15. Pineapple finial on the lid of a silver sauce tureen

16. Cauliflower knop on cover of silver dish

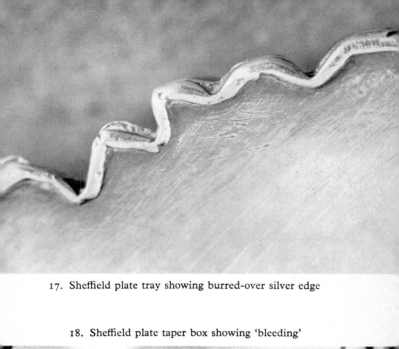

17. Sheffield plate tray showing burred-over silver edge

18. Sheffield plate taper box showing 'bleeding'

19. Transfer printing on a Dr Wall Worcester mug

20. The base of a Worcester mug showing glaze shrinkage where rim joins base

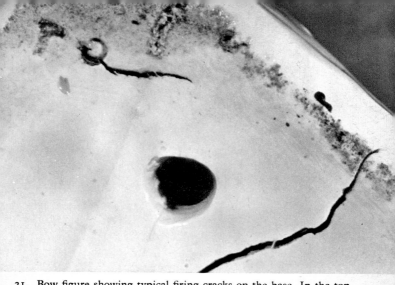

21. Bow figure showing typical firing cracks on the base. In the top left-hand corner are the impressed initials 'T.O.' said to be those of the famous modeller Tebo

22. Characteristic 'patch' marks on the base of a Chelsea-Derby figure made by the stands on which it stood in the kiln

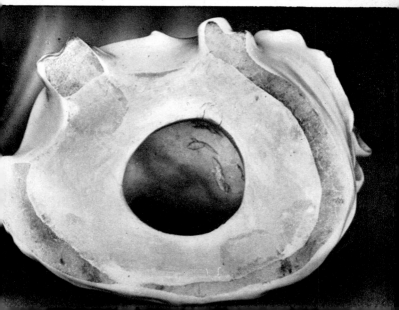

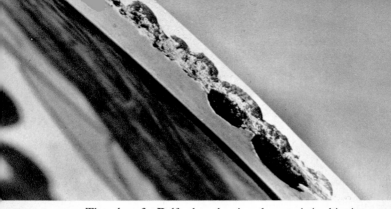

23. The edge of a Delft plate showing characteristic chipping

24. Bloor Derby figure of about 1820, six inches high

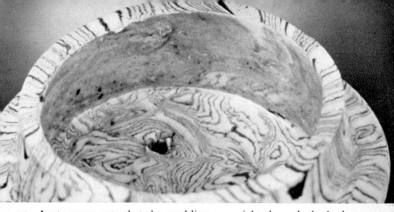

25. Agate ware: note that the marbling goes right through the body

26. Stem of a drinking glass with spiral twist

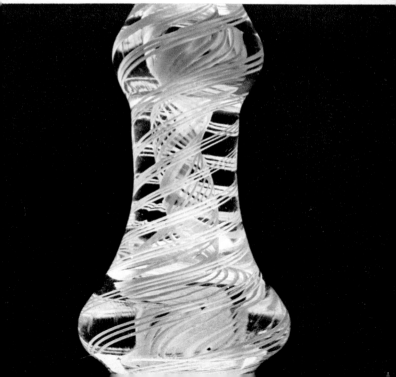

27. Base of an eighteenth-century drinking glass showing typical wear

28. Face of a Victorian automaton doll

29. Faked bruising on reproduction furniture, probably done with a bicycle chain

30. An inkstain purposely made on the inside of a drawer of a piece of faked furniture

31. A Chelsea Red Anchor mark

32. A Worcester Crescent mark

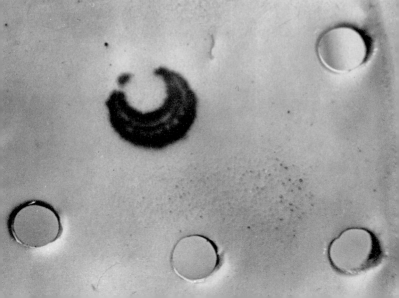

pottery and porcelain should carry the name of the country in which it was made.

2. The mark 'Bone China' was used after 1900. No antiques carry this description.

3. Some ceramics carry a registered number, sometimes printed, sometimes impressed, on a raised rectangular ribbon – eg, 'Rd No 265832'. Such numbers were only used after 1884.

4. Trade marks of limited liability companies which carry the mark 'Ltd' or 'Ld' are only found on ceramics made after 1860.

5. The words 'Trade Mark' appeared with the Trade Marks Act, which came into force in 1862, but were seldom used before 1875.

6. Beware of date marks included in a maker's mark: they nearly always indicate the date when the firm was first established, or even when its predecessor was established. The firm of George Jones & Sons of Stoke, for example, which operated from 1861 to 1952, shows the date 1790 on its 'Abbey' design mark which also includes the word 'England', indicating manufacture after 1891. Nineteenth-century porcelain from the Coalport factory often includes the date 1750 in its mark.

There are one or two other marks which help one to date nineteenth-century pieces. The word 'Royal' does not appear until after about 1850. The Worcester factory, for example, did not become the Worcester Royal Porcelain Works until 1862. The Royal Crown Derby Porcelain Company was formed in 1876.

Many Victorian pieces show a diamond-shaped pattern on the base which was used from 1842 when the Copyright Act came into force. This mark makes it possible to determine the actual year when a design was registered but does *not* give the actual date of manufacture, since designs were copyright for three years after registration. Fig 9 shows an actual mark. The 'IV' at the

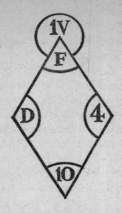

Figure 9   REGISTRATION MARK

The month letters were as follows:

C = Jan;   G = Feb;   W = Mar;   H = April;   E = May;   M = June;   I = July;   R = August;   D = Sept; B = Oct; K = Nov; A = Dec.

The year letters were

X	1842	P	1851	Z	1860
H	1843	D	1852	R	1861
C	1844	Y	1853	O	1862
A	1845	J	1854	G	1863
I	1846	E	1855	N	1864
F	1847	L	1856	W	1865
U	1848	K	1857	Q	1866
S	1849	B	1858	T	1867
V	1850	M	1859		

Figure 9 therefore indicates a pattern or design registered on September 4th, 1847.

apex of the diamond indicates the class of goods – in this case china and glass. The figure '4' on the right indicates the day of the month, the 'D' on the left the month, the 'F' at the top, the year, and the '10' at the bottom was a parcel number at the Patent Office. A code is needed to determine the month and year of registration since the letters of the alphabet were not used consecutively.

From 1867 to 1883 a new mark was used with the information differently distributed on the diamond, but it need not concern us here: details with the code are available in all good dictionaries of marks. The most comprehensive and up-to-date is the *Encyclopaedia of British Pottery and Porcelain Marks* by G. A. Godden (Herbert Jenkins). A useful book to carry around is a *Pocket Book of English Ceramic Marks,* compiled by J. P. Cushion (Faber and Faber).

Although marks can be a useful guide, do not rely too much on them, particularly if they are on fine porcelain. They can easily be copied or added to, and often were. The Derby factory, for example, produced many porcelain figures which bore the Meissen factory mark of blue crossed swords. On less expensive ware, and certainly on pottery, more reliance can be placed on the mark since it would seldom be worthwhile to fake such a piece.

The range of items available to the collector of earthenware or pottery is enormous. We can deal briefly only with one or two types and have chosen transfer ware, pot lids, earthenware figures, Mocha ware and what has come to be known as 'art pottery'.

Transfer Ware

Thomas Turner's introduction of transfer printing (p 68) saw the beginning of mass production in the pottery industry, which resulted in a flood of printed earthenware. Almost every pottery in the country produced this ware and much of it was of rather poor quality. The interest to the collector lies in its availability and in the attractive designs and colours of some of the finer pieces. Many of the early designs were direct copies of those on imported Chinese ware or were 'in the Chinese taste'. Of these, the willow pattern, still in use today, has probably been the most popular. It is thought to have been first engraved by Thomas Minton at the Caughley factory in 1780. Subsequently, he worked as a freelance copperplate engraver and produced variations on the Caughley design for use in other potteries, notably those of Spode and Adams. Many other engravers copied this design but they all differ considerably from the 'three men on the bridge' pattern now in use, which appears to have become the standard pattern by the middle of the nineteenth century.

Romantic designs with classical ruins became popular early in the nineteenth century. The best known is perhaps Spode's 'Italian' design, introduced in 1816 and still being used today. Some makers produced series with English or American views, though the latter were for export and are rarely seen in Britain and even specimens of the English series are hard to come by. Their makers included Adams, J. & R. Clews, R. Hall, Charles Meigh, Pountney & Allies, John & James Rogers, Andrew & Ralph Stevenson, and Enoch Wood & Sons.

Some of the most interesting designs were those based on engravings taken from books which were popular at the time. Sydney B. Williams carried out some valuable research on the origin of the Spode designs and the results were published in his *Antique Blue and White Spode*. He reveals that some of these designs were adapted from *Oriental Field Sports* (1805), a book dealing with the story of the hunt in India – a country which aroused much interest in the early nineteenth century; others proved to be from Mayer's *Views in Asia Minor* (1803) and Merigot's *Views and Ruins in Rome* (1798). Later, William Ridgway, Son & Co based designs for a dinner service on Hablot Browne's illustrations for *The Old Curiosity Shop*. This book was first serialized in a magazine called *Master Humphrey's Clock* and Ridgway used the words 'Humphrey's Clock' in his maker's mark. There were apparently insufficient suitable engravings in Dickens' book and so further engravings were made in a similar style. The partnership of Thomas and John Carey produced some superb quality blue and white ware with scenes illustrating Scott's *Lady of the Lake*, though we have not been able to trace that they were actually adapted from book engravings.

When buying these wares look at the quality of the transfer work. The skill acquired by the best transferrers was of a high standard and on the better-quality ware the joins in the pattern are hard to find. Except when ironstone was used, most early transfer pottery is light in weight compared with modern earthenware. The glaze of the early pieces has a characteristic ripple, rather like the surface of the sand on the seashore when the tide has gone out. Look also for the marks left by the spurs or stilts which supported each piece in the kiln and kept it from contact with its neighbour. These are usually three marks spaced round the back of each plate or dish, though occasionally they are found on the front, masked by the pattern. Many early plates have no base rim and show signs of constant wear.

Until 1842, when copyright protection became possible, designs were freely copied. It is therefore unwise to assume that a particular design was used only by the originator. Some people assert that each pottery had its own border pattern for its transfer ware and that these borders were not copied. Do not assume that this was always so, for there is much evidence to the contrary. Pountney & Allies of Bristol used border patterns which were also used by Spode and Rogers, and the border of the 'wild rose' pattern was used by at least three potteries – Bourne, Baker & Bourne of Fenton, Samuel Barker & Son of the Don Pottery, and by the Middlesbrough Pottery.

Pot Lids

At the beginning of the nineteenth century men had started to use oil and grease on their hair. Macassar oil from the East Indies was widely used (hence anti-macassars which the Victorians used to protect their up-holstered furniture from the oil), and bear grease was also popular. The latter was sold in round, white pomade pots and many of these were made by F. & R. Pratt & Co, of Fenton, a firm run by two brothers who employed a par-ticularly good decorator, Jesse Austin. Austin was not only a good artist but he had an inventive mind. By the time of the Great Exhibition in 1851, the firm had per-fected a process by which colour printing could be done by transfers, each colour being produced from a separate engraving. Decorated pot lids made by the Pratt factory have long been favourites with collectors. The firm of T. J. & J. Mayer is also known to have made pomade pots.

Hundreds of different pictures appear on early pot lids – rural scenes, animals, historic events, famous buildings, sports, and some are based on well-known oil paintings. These pots were certainly used for the sale of pomade, as well as fish and meat pastes, until about 1880. By then, they had become so popular with collectors that they were specially produced for this new market. Many of them were reproductions but a few were made using the original copper plates.

Collectors should bear the following points in mind.

1. The quality of the picture on a Pratt lid depended on

very accurate placing of the coloured transfers which had to be applied in sequence, one for each colour. Small marks (usually dots or circles) were printed on the edge of the designs to help accurate superimposition. Always look for these marks near the edge of the lid.

2. Some of the earliest lids, since the pots were intended for bear grease, bore scenes with bears, which covered the entire lid. These are now rather rare.

3. Many of the popular early pot lids have been reproduced in recent years. Sometimes these modern lids carry a mark stating that they are reproductions – but not always. The amateur will need to assess the character of the earthenware and glaze before deciding on the age of the lid.

4. Try to compare a known original with a reproduction pot lid. The colours on the early lids are stronger and the detail is finer.

5. Finally, carry out a 'ring' test. If the lid produces a ringing sound when struck lightly with a metal object it is probably a reproduction. If it produces a dull sound it is likely to be a genuine early specimen.

Earthenware Figures

Various names have been given to earthenware figures at different times. In the middle of the eighteenth century they were called image toys, by 1800 they were merely toys. Twenty years later they were being advertised as chimney ornaments and today they are usually referred to as Staffordshire figures, though they were undoubtedly also made in other parts of Britain.

Some of the earliest figures are associated with the Wood family. Ralph Wood (1717–72) was a particularly fine modeller noted for his coloured metallic glazes. Well-known examples of his work are 'The Vicar and Moses', 'Old Age', 'Diogenes looking for an Honest Man',

'Charity', and the 'Toby Philpot' jug. They were sometimes signed 'R. Wood' and were later widely copied. His
son, also a Ralph Wood (1748–95), continued the tradition and made many figures similar to those made by
his father, as well as some of his own design including
busts of Handel and Milton. Ralph Wood Jr did some of
his work in enamel: the colour was made to fuse with the
glaze by adding a glassy flux before firing. His work is
signed 'Ra. Wood'.

Enoch Wood, cousin of Ralph Jr, and more than ten
years younger, not only modelled figures but was a keen
collector of earthenware. John Wesley, when visiting the
Potteries, gave sittings to the young Enoch Wood, and the
bust he made has been much copied by other potters. By
the time he died in 1840 at the age of eighty-one, the
modelling of well-known figures had become very popular. In the early part of the nineteenth century, toys or
chimney ornaments and fairground pieces were turned
out from the potteries in their thousands. Among the
makers was John Walton whose figures are often backed
by a spreading tree with foliage, a convention known as
'bocage' which was popular on the early porcelain figures
made at the Bow and Chelsea factories. Another modeller
of the period was Obadiah Sherratt, who became known
for his bull-baiting group – a man with a staff, arms up-
raised, with dogs attacking a bull. He also made figures of
famous people such as Napoleon, Wellington and Nelson,
and milk jugs in the shape of a cow. It was jokingly said
in the Potteries that Sherratt used the same mould for a
cow's teat and Wellington's nose!

Other known figure-makers were J. Dale of Burslem,
Ralph Hall of Tunstall, Ralph Salt of Hanley and Felix
and R. Pratt of Fenton.

The manufacture of chimney ornaments continued
throughout the nineteenth century. Figures included royalty, wartime leaders, politicians, evangelists (Moody and

Sankey) and even criminals. Innumerable dogs were modelled, some sporting dogs, some lap dogs. Few can fail to
have seen the flat-faced hearth dogs, like a King Charles
spaniel, which were made in large numbers and have
been copied until quite recent times.

It is useful to know that the early figures were made by
hand. The clay was pressed into the moulds with the
fingers and the base was closed and recessed, though a
small hole was left somewhere in the figure to release
expanding air during firing. The colouring was often
crude, but vigorous, usually under the glaze. Later figures
were made by pouring a liquid slip into porous plaster
moulds. These acted as blotting paper, soaking up the
moisture from the slip which then slowly hardened.
These figures tend to be smoother, and may have an open
base and often a flat, undecorated back. Colours were applied sparingly (since the cream-glazed surface was attractive in itself), usually over the glaze. Gilding was
common.

Art Pottery

In the second half of the nineteenth century, when mass
production was the rule, individual London artists were
making and decorating various types of salt-glazed stoneware which has come to be known as art pottery. A great
deal was made at the Doulton factory at Lambeth and
some by the four Martin brothers at a small pottery at
Southall. Many collectors now show a great interest in
this ware. About one hundred years ago the Doulton factory, always well-known for its brown, salt-glazed ware
decorated with hunting scenes in relief, started to employ
individual artists, mainly young women who had been
trained at the Lambeth School of Art, as decorators. The
artist was able to select the stoneware piece she wished to
work on and was free to use her own individual style of

decoration. This was usually incised on the body and was hand coloured before firing. The vases, jugs, cups and candlesticks so produced found a ready market and within ten years of the beginning of this experiment Doulton's were employing over 200 artists, many of whom gained a considerable reputation. These decorators included Hannah, Florence and Arthur Barlow, Frank Butler, Mark Marshall, Eliza Simmance and George Tinworth. It is a field to be recommended for the amateur collector. All the pieces carry the name of the factory, the artist's mark and a date mark. The artists' marks are listed in several books of marks. This Doulton ware is increasing in value.

While these developments were taking place in the Doulton factory, four brothers by the name of Martin set up a factory at Southall in 1877 and, by dint of steady application and much laborious experiment, succeeded in producing a salt-glazed stoneware of fine quality, despite being handicapped by lack of both experience and capital. They loved their work and made themselves familiar with every process of their art which, as a result, was highly individual. It was more expensive than mass-produced ware and was bought privately, mainly by collectors. There was no business organization in the ordinary sense of the word. The organizer was Charles Martin who, after twenty years' work with his brothers and despite a dislike of publicity, was persuaded in 1897 to give an interview to a journalist working for *The Ludgate* magazine. He explained their policy thus:

So as to separate ourselves as far as possible from the manufacturers who turn out similar pieces by the hundred, we make it a matter of pride never to repeat a single specimen of our work. Even in the case of a pair of vases, you will find that the design, though of similar character, differs materially on each specimen . . . each

of our designs is original and never repeated. They
have to be engraved or etched, when the clay is
sufficiently set, with some hard point, generally steel.
The clay is then so hard that a line once made cannot
be obliterated, but must be included in the design.

The output of the Martin brothers consisted largely of
shaped bowls, jugs and vases, and of grotesque figures of
animals, fish and birds (particularly owls). Much of the
work has unusual colouring for this kind of stoneware.
Most of their pieces are signed and dated. The brothers
were so engrossed in their work that money meant little
to them and they kept many of their finer specimens for
their own collection – most of these, fortunately, have
since found their way into museums. The Martin-ware
pottery collection is housed in the public library in Os-
terley Park Road, Southall, Middlesex.

Mocha Ware

Throughout the nineteenth century, mugs, jugs and other
useful containers were produced cheaply in potteries all
over Britain in a cream or white earthenware with a strik-
ing, tree-like decoration. This Mocha ware, as it is called,
was used in public houses, markets and poorer homes,
though there was also an export trade. The basic decoration is in coloured bands running around the body,
usually of brown, blue or grey, with narrow black bands
between them. The widest band is in the middle of the
article and black, feathery shapes spread upwards on this
band. The coloured bands were applied as slip while the
dried pot was spinning on a lathe. The pot was then
placed upside down while the slip was still wet and blobs
of dark-coloured 'tea', said to have been made from hops
and tobacco juice, were dabbed on near the upper edge of
the widest band. This 'tea' then spread outward through

the coloured slip to form tree-like fronds.

Mocha jugs can still be seen in the bars of old inns and many of them carry a raised crown mark in white with the word 'IMPERIAL' on a ribbon beneath, showing that they have been approved as measures by the Weights and Measures Authority. Sometimes the marks are printed on the body of the vessel and sometimes on a metal button fitted into a hole.

The amateur earthenware collector may wish to specialize in one type of pottery, or even in the products of a single factory, or he may like to cover a wide range of wares, collecting a specimen of each. In either case, it is wise to consider at an early stage the problems of display and storage. Plates look well on a Welsh dresser, on a high ledge around a room, or even resting on top of a wooden pelmet. Mugs or jugs need a shelf or windowsill, and a collection of these can look most attractive.

CHAPTER EIGHT

GLASS

GLASS vessels of various kinds have been made for centuries and much Roman glass still exists. In England, although glass was certainly made in Tudor times, the industry only became firmly established in the second half of the seventeenth century. This resulted from experiments carried out by George Ravenscroft, who discovered that lead oxide added in fairly large quantities to the molten glass greatly improved its quality and made it possible to produce an excellent glass that also showed more sparkle.

The variety of objects made from glass is enormous. Not only are there hundreds of types of drinking glasses and of bottles, jugs and decanters to hold the liquor, but all manner of tableware has been and is still being made – sugar basins, salt cellars, sweet dishes, cups for custard and dessert, cream jugs, finger-bowls, cake-stands, fruit bowls, candlesticks, epergnes . . . the list is endless. In this chapter, we shall deal with transparent or crystal-glass drinking glasses and decanters made in the eighteenth and nineteenth centuries, and with a few of the many types of coloured glass.

Drinking Glasses

When trying to date a drinking glass it is necessary to study the bowl, the stem and the foot. Even then it is seldom possible to place it within narrow time limits because many shapes and styles persisted over long periods.

It is possible, however, to state when a particular style was most popular.

Until well into the eighteenth century, English drinking glasses were usually fairly large and heavy in contrast to the Venetian glass which had previously been popular. They nearly always had a greenish-grey colour, as it was not until the middle of the eighteenth century that ways were found of bleaching glass.

Let us first consider the bowls of drinking glasses. At the end of the seventeenth century these were mainly *funnel-shaped* (Fig 10a), or *fluted* (Fig 10d) but other shapes were evolving which gained great popularity in the eighteenth century. First came the *bell-shaped* (Fig 10b) and *waisted* (Fig 10c) bowls and a little later the *trumpet* (Fig 10e) bowl – an early shape which had been out of favour for a long time. Between 1715 and 1720, new shapes emerged, the *thistle-shaped* bowl (Fig 10f) and the *straight-sided* glass (Fig 10g) of which large numbers were made, probably for serving gin in inns. Just before 1750, new bowl shapes were introduced known as the *ogee* bowl (Fig 10h) and the *double ogee* bowl (Fig 10i). Then came the *bucket* bowl (Fig 10j) and its variant the *waisted-bucket*, which remained popular until about 1775. The seventeenth-century *round funnel* bowl produced its variant, thinned down and extended (Fig 10k). Throughout the eighteenth century glasses had become thinner and finer but the vogue for etched engraving and cut ornamentation towards the end of the period made it necessary to produce a slightly thicker glass again. The *ovoid* bowl (Fig 10l) appeared. In the nineteenth century, there were no startling new bowl shapes: existing types were modified to suit prevailing fashions.

When dating a glass, the stem is often more significant than the bowl it supports, and so are shaped enlargements in the stem which are known as knops. The shapes of

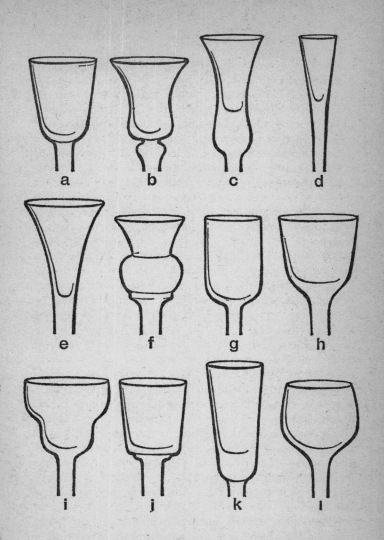

Figure 10 DRINKING GLASSES: BOWLS

stems and knops varied enormously and the periods when each style was being made overlapped. We give the main types below with the period during which they were in fashion.

1. The *Baluster* (Fig 11a) was popular from about 1685 to the 1720s though it was still made up to about 1760. It is usually found in the inverted form (Fig 11b) and, after 1720, often with knops above or below the baluster. The drawn stems often include a bubble or tear.

2. The *Drawn Plain* stems often include a bubble or tear (Fig 11c). They were turned out in their thousands because they were easy to make. Though first seen in the seventeenth century, they appear to have been out of favour until about 1715. By 1740, they were well established and were widely used for the next thirty years or more.

3. The *Moulded Pedestal* (Fig 11d) was first made about 1715 and lasted well past the middle of the century. Four-, six- and eight-sided varieties are known. It is sometimes known as the *Silesian* stem.

4. *Air Twist* stems (Fig 11e) were probably a direct challenge to the plain stem and many consider them an entirely English creation. They appeared in various forms between 1730 and 1770.

5. The *Opaque Twist* is similar in appearance to the Air Twist but the columns were of enamel instead of air. The twist was often white but colours were used after 1765. Their popularity waned after 1780.

6. The *Incised Twist* (Fig 11f) was only made for a short period round about 1750: these stems are rare.

7. *Faceted* stems (Fig 11g) involved cut decoration. Various types of facet were cut into the glass in a regular pattern. They were made from about 1760 until the early nineteenth century.

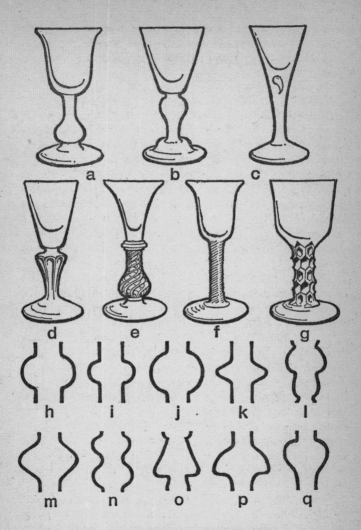

Figure 11   DRINKING GLASSES:
STEMS AND KNOPS

Figure 12 DRINKING GLASS FEET AND DECANTER STOPPERS

After 1800, stems began to disappear and short stemless glasses gained favour.

The knops which appear in the stems of glasses usually take their name from their shape. They include the *Plain* knop (Fig 11h), *Flattened* knop (Fig 11i), *Ball* knop (Fig 11j), *Bladed* knop (Fig 11k), *Acorn* knop (Fig 11l), *Wide Angular* knop (Fig 11m), *Dumb Bell* knop (Fig 11n), *Drop* knop (Fig 11o), *Mushroom* knop (Fig 11p) and *Shoulder* knop (Fig 11q).

The foot of a glass does not lend itself to so many variations as the bowl and the stem. There are, however, several well defined types:

1. The *Conical* foot (Fig 12a) found in both plain and solid form.

2. The *Folded* foot (Fig 12b), so called because the outer rim is doubled back under itself, a form which gave the foot tremendous strength. It is more likely to break completely than to chip but a good deal of force is needed to shatter it. The domed or bracket folded foot (Fig 12c) is a variant.

3. The *Firing* foot (Fig 12d) is a heavy, strong foot about a quarter of an inch thick, so called because it produced a loud sound like gunfire when banged on a table as a toasting glass.

In the early nineteenth century, the *Rummer* (Fig 12e) was probably the most popular type of glass. It gets its name from the German *Roemer* (meaning Roman), although it was often used to serve rum drinks.

When buying old glasses, examine the base carefully. When a glass is blown a sharp and jagged surface is left where it is snapped from the pipe. This is known as the pontil mark and will be found on the base of most glasses made before about 1750. After this date the makers began to grind the mark away. Few nineteenth-century glasses retain their pontil mark.

The bases of old glasses usually show scratches due to wear over long periods (see Illus. 27). Scratching can be faked by rubbing the base of a glass with emery paper or a rough stone. Examine the scratching very carefully: faked scratches are often curved where the forger used a circular action with the abrasive.

Glasses which have been chipped are sometimes ground down and repolished. This destroys the proportions of the glass: the ground parts look too small for the rest. If the top rim has been ground it may have a flattened surface (Fig 12g) instead of the normal rounded one (Fig 12f).

Decanters

Many families have an old decanter among their inherited possessions, and these are much easier to date than drinking glasses. The shape of the body, neck and stopper of the decanter evolved in an orderly sequence, though many decanters have unfortunately lost their original or period stoppers. Many dealers and collectors hoard old stoppers in the hope of matching them to decanters which are incomplete.

During the first quarter of the eighteenth century, heavy-based decanters were popular. They are known as *Mallet* decanters (Fig 13a) and were usually six- or eight-sided, though they were sometimes cruciform with the body lobed in the shape of a cross (Fig 13b). The necks of these decanters were usually at least as tall as the body. A ring of glass was moulded around the top of the neck, so that string could be tied round the neck without slipping. Such rings certainly prevent a decanter from slipping through the fingers. In some cases there is more than one ring of glass. The *Shaft* and *Globe* decanter (Fig 13c) was also produced in this period. This was simply blown and looked rather like a bulbous bottle. The same shape

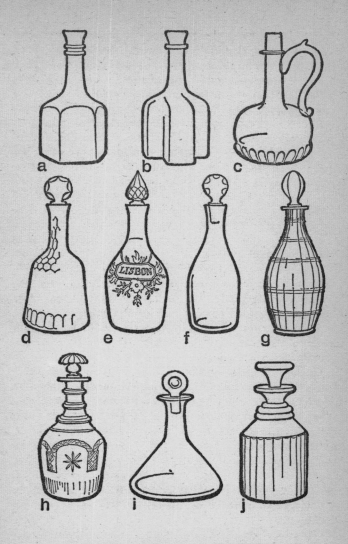

Figure 13 DECANTER SHAPES

became popular again in the Regency period. Early eighteenth-century decanter stoppers were usually ball-shaped
and are not ground where they fit into the neck.

Decanters with broad (Fig 13e) or narrow (Fig 13d)
shoulders had appeared by about 1740. They quickly
gained in popularity and persisted into the nineteenth
century. These were the first decanters to be decorated by
cutting and gilding. Taper decanters with lozenge-shaped
stoppers were popular during the 1760s and were also
made well into the nineteenth century (Fig 13f). Decanters engraved or gilded with imitation wine labels and
chains (Fig 13e) appeared at about the same time and
were popular again in Regency times. They were also
made in coloured glass (see page 108). Decanters shaped
like a barrel (Fig 13g) were used during the last quarter of
the eighteenth century.

Early nineteenth-century decanters include the Prussian and cylindrical types. In the *Prussian* decanter (Fig
13h) the bulbous body slopes in gently to the base. These
usually have several rings set around the neck, and a
mushroom-shaped stopper. The *Cylindrical* decanter
(Fig 13j) has a straight-sided body decorated with vertical
flutes and a ringed neck.

A special kind of decanter appeared in the 1780s which
was designed for use on board ship. They were made with
wide, heavy bases which made it almost impossible to
turn them over. These ship's decanters (Fig 13i) which
are sometimes called 'Rodneys' are much sought after.

It may be helpful to list and date some of the commoner types of decanter stopper. They include:

The *Ball Finial* (Fig 12h), early eighteenth century.
The *Vertical Lozenge* (Fig 12i), mid to late eighteenth
century.
The *Pear-Shaped* (Fig 12j), late eighteenth century.
The *Mushroom* (Fig 12k) and the *Target* (Fig 12l), late

eighteenth and early nineteenth century.

The *Cut Globe* (Fig 12m), early nineteenth century.

The Ball Finial was decorated with air bubbles after about 1710 and with tear-shaped bubbles from about 1720. Stoppers and the inner surfaces of decanter necks were ground about 1745 to ensure a good air-tight fit, and the bottoms of stoppers were ground flat and polished.

COLOURED GLASS

Coloured glass was first made in quantity in the second half of the eighteenth century, partly because the duty on clear crystal glass had been increased, partly in an attempt to compete with something 'new' against the large quantities of Chinese porcelain then entering the country. It is not surprising, therefore, that the glassmakers should attempt to produce an opaque white glass as a direct rival to imported porcelain. This was achieved at Bristol and much of it was decorated 'in the Chinese taste', as was early English porcelain, though some appears to have been sent to Liverpool to be transfer printed. The only artist to have been identified as a decorator of this early white glass was Michael Edkins. Although this type of glass tends to be described as 'Bristol' glass, it is now certain that it was also made elsewhere in England during this period. Fine specimens cost a great deal of money: it is not a field for the collector of moderate means.

The name 'Bristol' is even more frequently associated with a deep blue, transparent glass, though similar glass was also made in the Midlands and the north-east of England. Many people think of 'Bristol Blue' as a type of glass. It is not. 'Bristol Blue' is a colour. The name probably derives from the fact that the finest smalt, the raw material which contained the cobalt colouring, was imported into Bristol for distribution to glassworks all over the country. The blue glass actually made in Bristol seems to have been of such high quality that other manufacturers were anxious to imitate it, but it is doubtful whether even a glass expert could identify with certainty the place of manufacture of a piece of eighteenth-century blue glass. The amateur will find more interest in the style and decoration of the articles than in quibbling about the origin of the glass itself.

Decanters are the commonest 'Bristol' glass to be seen today. They were made long and tapering with a lozenge-shaped stopper; others were shouldered and were made in sets, each bottle bearing the name of the liquid it was to hold gilded on the glass, sometimes with a gilded chain added as though a wine label had been hung from the neck. Although the quality of the glass was good, the gilding was often poor and is frequently badly worn. A very few pieces of old Bristol glass are actually signed: 'I. Jacob, Bristol'. These, at least, are known to be authentic but beware of the single word 'Bristol' on blue glass. Modern glass made in central Europe is sometimes marked in this way.

The Nailsea glassworks established near Bristol in 1788 also gave its name to a type of coloured glassware that was made in other parts of the country. Its major output seems to have been after the tax on glass was lifted in 1845. It specialized in what have come to be known as 'friggers' – curiosities made in glass, like image toys in earthenware, probably for sale at country fairs. They include handbells, walking sticks, pipes, pocket flasks and hollow rolling pins which, legend has it, were given to sailors to use for smuggling tea into the country. The flasks and the bowls of the pipes often show festooning in white and coloured threads running through the clear glass. A special type of filigree work was said to have been done by French craftsmen working at Nailsea, and sometimes tiny glass top hats turn up which are thought to have been apprentice pieces. The Nailsea factory ceased to operate in 1873.

In Victorian times, new techniques were used to make glass articles, and in this connexion it is useful to be able to distinguish between moulded glass and mechanically-pressed glass. Moulded glass is blown into the mould and any fluting or corrugation on the outside of the moulded glass has a corresponding fluting or corrugation inside. Except in the case of articles which would slip out of a mould without the need to open it, one can usually trace on the surface of the glass the faint thin mark where the sections of the mould met. Very often, the rim of the object was ground flat. On this type of moulded glass there is no pontil mark unless, of course, a glassblower worked on the piece after moulding.

Pressed glass was made by forcing the molten glass into a metal mould by pressing it down with a shaped plunger. In this case, only the outside of the glass object received the pattern from the mould, the inside taking the smooth surface of the plunger or whatever pattern the plunger itself may have imposed.

Although pressed glass was made as early as the 1820s, the output was relatively small until about 1870, when three glass factories in the north-east of England produced large quantities. These were Sowerby & Company of Gateshead, Greener & Company of Sunderland, and George Davidson & Company of Gateshead. The latter made a most attractive type of glass known as 'Pearline', in which a clear coloured glass dies away into a pearly white glass. Some pressed glass is known as 'lace glass' because of its delicate patterns. Lace glass was sometimes used for commemorative pieces. An excellent account of late Victorian pressed glass is given in Mr G. A. Godden's *Antique China and Glass under £5* (Barker, 1966).

A number of other types of Victorian glass deserve mention.

1. *Burmese* glass, despite its name, has no connexion with Burma. It is a translucent unpolished glass which shades from semi-opaque flesh-pink into a pale yellow colour. It was first patented by the Mt Washington Glass Company of America in 1885, and manufactured under licence by Thomas Webb & Sons of Stourbridge in the following year. Queen Victoria became very interested in this glass which was later known as *Queen's Burmese*. It is highly valued.

2. *Cameo* glass was produced in the 1880s by a process developed by John Northwood nearly twenty years earlier. A rich-coloured glass was coated with white enamel on which a design was etched, cut or carved. By dissolving unwanted enamel with hydrofluoric acid, the design was made to stand out boldly against a coloured background. Cameo glass is greatly prized by collectors and fetches high prices.

3. *Cased* glass involved fusing one or more layers of coloured glass over clear flint glass. By cutting the outer layer or layers, the clear glass was revealed. This cutting was sometimes done to create panels of clear glass which could be decorated with applied enamels. Cased glass is often known as overlay glass.

4. *Cranberry* glass is a name given by Americans to what is often called 'ruby glass', though it varies a good deal in depth of colour. This red glassware was popular in early Victorian times and was made until about 1900. The earlier pieces are of blown glass: later pieces were often pressed. It was widely used for tableware and for every possible kind of decorative article – glasses, decanters, jugs, finger bowls, custard cups, sugar sifters, rose bowls, vases, epergnes, and powder bowls. Vases and glasses may have a clear-glass base, jugs and decanters

clear-glass handles, and most decorative pieces carry pinched clear-glass ornamentation. Seen against plain walls, preferably with the lighting behind them, cranberry glass pieces add a warm richness to any room but, except for a few particularly fine or unusual specimens, they will not provide much excitement for the collector. Cranberry glass is, at the moment, too plentiful.

5. *Opal* glass, or *Opaline*, was a milky-white glass made by the addition of arsenic. It is recognized by the fiery glow seen when viewed against a strong light. In the 1870s, coloured opaline appeared in delicate shades of yellow, green and blue. The coloured vases were often painted with sprays of flowers or other ornamentation.

6. *Spatter* glass was made by gathering up small blobs of coloured glass on a larger mass of opaque white or cream-coloured glass before blowing into a mould. The resulting article has a surface spattered or streaked with several bright colours, but the inside is pure white or cream.

7. *Vaseline* glass is, as its name implies, a pale, golden-green colour which, especially in later examples, may show a pearly cloudiness in places.

THE CARE OF GLASS

Glass should be washed in clean soapy water, rinsed in warm water and dried on a linen cloth. Never immerse glass in very hot water.

One of the most difficult problems is the decanter. When they have not been used for some time a white chalky deposit may often be seen over the inside surface and there may be a ring of thicker deposit where the liquid it contained evaporated from the surface. This white deposit is not easily removed and can seldom be washed away. There are, however, some time-honoured tips which are useful: this 'hint to servants' in *The Young Housewife's Daily Assistant* of 1864 is still valid. 'Decanters should be cleaned with tea leaves and a bottle brush, and well rinsed with cold water, then turned upside down to drain. Be careful never to use soda, or any acid, it makes them look thick, cloudy and white, instead of clear and brilliant.'

Another method is to put several dozen dried peas into the decanter and to swill them round and round with water, but to date the most satisfactory method we have found is to obtain fine lead shot and to swill this around in the same way.

The removal of decanter stoppers which are stuck is always a problem. Try filling a deep bowl or bucket with hot water into which you can put your hand with comfort. Place the body of the decanter, including the neck, upright in the water, making sure that no part of the stopper is in contact with the hot water. Keep up a steady twisting action on the stopper as though you were continually turning a tap on and off. At the moment when the heat has expanded the glass of the neck but has not yet reached the stopper, the latter should be released. If this does not happen the first time, allow the decanter to cool down completely before trying again.

Valuable glass occasionally gets chipped. If this unfortunately happens, a small chip can be removed by careful grinding and polishing – a job which must be done by an expert glazier. This does, of course, seriously diminish its value but it does mean that it can be kept for display as an example of its period, or because of its beauty.

Photographers should be warned when recording rare pieces that considerable heat is radiated by a photographic lamp and it should not be allowed near a glass object for more than a few seconds at a time. Many fine glasses have been shattered before the camera.

Some Victorian glass bottles and decanters have a metal mount around the rim, secured to the glass with a mixture of plaster and size: never immerse such articles in water.

Coloured Victorian glass is often decorated with clear-glass ornamentation. This can sometimes act as a lens in sunlight, concentrating the rays on the main body and causing it to crack. In hot, sunny weather, such articles should be kept away from the direct rays of the sun.

CHAPTER NINE

ORIENTAL ANTIQUES

ORIENTAL antiques are usually regarded as those
which have come from the Far East – from China
and Japan. Chinese porcelain is world famous, and
rightly so. It was probably being made at least a century
before the birth of Christ, and by the thirteenth century
the Chinese were making fine quality wares in considerable quantity. Their porcelain was of a hard-paste
type not made in England until Cookworthy discovered
the secret of manufacturing a similar paste at Plymouth in
1768.

The word 'Ming' is often lightly and wrongly used by
amateurs to describe Oriental ware. In fact, the name
signifies a dynasty covering nearly three hundred years,
from 1368 to 1643. The oldest examples of Chinese porcelain one may now hope to find come from this period,
though the chances of doing so are very slight: even
though a piece may look 'right' and be correctly marked,
it is very unlikely to be genuine. Chinese potters have
always copied the great patterns and marks of the past
and continue to do so today. Most Chinese porcelain to be
found in shops was made in the nineteenth century, but
the most fruitful period to which hopeful collectors may
look is the Chien Lung period from 1736 to 1795. This
porcelain, if held in a certain light, often reveals a surface
pitted like the skin of an orange.

The symbols used by the Chinese when decorating
their porcelain are of great interest. The *Bat* (which often
looks like a pair of elephant's heads complete with trunks)
was their symbol of happiness. The *Dragon* with five

claws was the Imperial emblem: with four claws it indicated royal blood, and with three claws, nobility. *Two Fish* signified married bliss. A plant looking rather like a vase with two leaves projecting from the neck, called the *Che plant*, was the sign of longevity, as was the *Hare*. The *Rabbit* was the sign of fertility, and the *Leaf* an emblem of goodness. These were often incorporated in the decorative designs on porcelain and were sometimes used as marks.

Chinese porcelain is also famous for its *Famille Verte* and *Famille Rose* wares. These names refer to a predominance of a single colour – green or a delicate rose-pink. *Famille Noire* (black) and *Famille Jaune* (yellow) are also found, but rarely.

During the eighteenth century, which covers the Chien Lung period, the trade routes between Europe and China were numerous and tea was one of the main commodities. The Chinese took this opportunity to produce great quantities of porcelain for the European markets and one type, known as armorial, bears the coats-of-arms of families in England. Services were specially ordered and drawings of the crests or coats-of-arms were sent with the order for the Chinese artists to copy. Chinese armorial porcelain fetches very high prices. Another type of eighteenth-century Oriental decoration is known as 'Jesuit'. The designs – often with a religious motif – were usually executed in black and gold. Some of this porcelain was commissioned by Jesuit priests in China. Only study, experience and constant handling will enable a new collector to learn to distinguish between old and new Chinese porcelain.

Many people either own or come across old Chinese bronze vessels. Most of these were made in the nineteenth century to sell to unsuspecting tourists. A genuine old Chinese bronze is usually covered with an emerald-green patina. This is so hard that a fingernail scraped across it has no effect. Many of the later copies have had this green layer artificially added, but it is soft and can be scraped away with the nail.

The Chinese were not noted for outstanding work with precious metals and silver and gold are seldom seen in their artistic work. They did, however, make magnificent objects in jade, a natural translucent mineral varying in colour from almost white to many shades of green. It was too hard to carve and had to be worn into shape by constant rubbing with an abrasive. True jade is so hard that if a knife edge is run across it, the knife will be blunted without making any impression on the jade. True jade is also ice-cold to the touch no matter what the temperature of the surrounding air. This is why an expert will test a jade object by touching it with the tip of his tongue, or holding it against his forehead.

Cloisonné enamel work was made famous by the Chinese. Thin wires were soldered to the body of a metal vessel to form the design. The decoration was then split up with more wires to form little cells which were then filled with different coloured enamels. An old piece of *cloisonné* may often be distinguished from later specimens by the small blobs of solder seen where the wires meet each other, though this is not an infallible criterion. Old *cloisonné* also tends to be heavier than the more modern pieces.

Carved red lacquer was used by the Chinese to decorate boxes and small cabinets, though it has also been used on large pieces of furniture. The surface of the article to be decorated was covered with a thin layer of bright red lacquer. This was allowed to dry until completely hard and then another coat and another was added, until perhaps one hundred or more layers had been built up. The thick rubbery surface was then delicately carved. When looked at under a magnifying glass, the layers which have been cut through can be distinctly seen looking like the edges of a closed book. Sometimes several

colours of enamel were used, beginning with layers of one
colour and continuing with layers of another. This gave
the carving a relief effect. Black and red were a common
combination. The many nineteenth-century copies of this
lacquer can easily be detected: the article to be decorated
was coated with a thick layer of clay which was carved
and then covered with a single coating of red lacquer.
The general appearance is much softer because of the
rounded outlines and no telltale layers can be seen under
a magnifying glass. A pin carefully stuck into the object
will reveal the clay when pulled out.

Japan

Porcelain made in Japan has never seemed to appeal as
widely as Chinese porcelain. It is certainly regarded by
many as being some way behind in quality. Perhaps the
most famous of all Japanese ware is *Imari*, named after
the port from which it was exported. The decoration is in
dark reds and blues with some gilding. The early *Imari*
porcelain was of good quality but much *Imari* ware exported to Europe late in the nineteenth century was not
so good: smaller pieces of this can still be bought for a
matter of shillings. The larger vases, however, are now
fetching higher prices.

The porcelain of Japan may have lacked artistic merit
but the skill of the Japanese carvers in ivory has never
been surpassed. Japanese clothing had no pockets: people
usually carried a small box with drawstrings to keep it
closed and to suspend it from the wearer's belt. The
toggle which secured the strings to the belt was known as
a *netsuke*. *Netsuke* were usually made of ivory, bone or
wood, and were nearly always delicately carved. Among
the finest are those in the form of a mushroom with
deeply carved gills. Great skill and craftsmanship was required for this work and artists became famous for the

originality and execution of their carvings. Most of the finer *netsuke* were made in the eighteenth and early nineteenth century and were often signed by the craftsmen who carved them. Towards the end of the nineteenth century, however, European clothing increased in popularity and fewer *netsuke* were made. It was not long, however, before they were being sought by collectors as minor works of art and this new demand eventually became so great that they were actually made again purely to sell to collectors. Today, beautifully carved and signed early *netsuke* fetch high prices at auction.

Japanese prints or, strictly speaking, woodcuts, have a grace, charm and simplicity of line unequalled in the history of art. (Copperplate printing did not come to Japan until the nineteenth century.) In the seventeenth and eighteenth centuries many coloured woodcuts were produced which have been eagerly purchased whenever offered for sale. The recognition of these early woodcuts is a job for the specialist. Realizing the demand for them, Japanese artists have recut the original blocks many times and have cut many exact copies in order to meet it. Often, only careful comparison with a known early version makes it possible to date one of these prints. To the trained eye, the later versions are stiffer and lack the flow of the originals. This is not surprising. If you take a pencil and draw a waving line on a piece of paper it comes naturally and quickly. Now copy this line exactly. This will need some care and, because of the lack of flow, it will look stiff and harsh in comparison with the original, however well executed.

The Japanese were also noted for their skill in making arms, particularly swords and armour, but this is a very specialized field.

CHAPTER TEN

ANTIQUES FOR THE WALL

ALL kinds of antiques can be used to decorate interior walls – oil paintings, water-colour drawings, old prints and maps, miniatures, silhouettes, needlework pictures, samplers, decorative plates and weapons. Each one could provide study for a lifetime: we can do no more here than give a few notes on each which may help the prospective buyer to explore the field in more detail.

In the nineteenth century, painting in oils and water colours was a common accomplishment or pastime. Thousands of people fancied their skill. Today, the pictures they painted are scattered throughout the antique and bric-à-brac shops of Britain and there are few auction rooms where paintings are not offered for sale. Most of them are by unknown, unrecognized amateur artists and as such seldom command high prices, though some are attractive enough to hang on the wall. As John Ruskin said: 'They are good furniture pictures, unworthy of praise, and undeserving of blame'. This is a field in which personal taste is all important. If you like a picture well enough to live with it, it can be a good buy. It may even appreciate in value. Tastes change and a previously unknown artist may suddenly come into fashion. Many pictures by Victorian artists which would have attracted little attention a few years ago are now being bought for quite high prices.

Always be a little suspicious when buying a signed picture. Many artists whose work now commands a good price were copied and most of the copies bear a faked signature. Some auctioneers have a catalogue convention to deal with this situation. If they are quite certain that a picture is genuine they will print the artist's name in full – eg, 'Edwin Landseer'. If the catalogue simply states that the picture is by 'E. Landseer', it may only mean that the picture is attributed to Landseer. The name 'Landseer' alone, without christian name or initial, means that the picture is possibly not genuine: it has probably been painted by some unknown artist 'in the manner of Landseer'. Today, some unscrupulous people are buying cheap pictures of certain categories – landscapes and seascapes, for example – and are painting on to these the signatures of well-known artists in the hope that unwary picture buyers may think they are getting a bargain. So be warned. The amateur would be very unwise to buy an expensive picture without the prior opinion of an art expert.

Many old paintings are too large for the wall of a modern home and the smaller ones tend to fetch relatively higher prices. For this reason, old prints provide an attractive alternative. They are seldom very large and those that have originated as book plates, even when framed with a mount, will seldom be more than a foot in width. Many people like prints in colour and for this reason black and white engravings are often tinted or coloured before they are offered for sale. However, it is still possible to obtain early colour prints relatively cheaply, especially if they are bought unframed. We have recently seen prints by famous caricaturists of the late eighteenth and early nineteenth centuries offered in antique shops for less than £1 each and it is sometimes possible to pick up an old and worn book with prints which can be used, though we do not recommend the 'breaking' of well-bound complete volumes for the sake of the prints. It is often done, but it is sacrilege to the book-lover.

Look out for coloured prints by Rowlandson

(1756–1827), who was a great traveller in the heyday of the stage-coach and loved the English inn. He had a fertile imagination and a light touch: his illustrations for the *Tours of Dr Syntax* are delightful and can still be found. James Gillray (1737–1815), a friend of Rowlandson, is known for his broad satirical humour aimed mainly at Napoleon, George III and the main political figures of his day.

Coloured sporting and equestrian prints, especially those by well-known artists such as H. Alken and J. F. Herring Sr, are much sought after, especially by horse-riding and hunting enthusiasts. They were usually produced in sets of four or six and these can fetch £50 or more for a set, though single prints cost relatively less.

Black and white prints are more easily come by: they are to be found in many old topographical books and in the 1830s it was fashionable to bind up the illustrations engraved for the books of famous authors in separate volumes; Finden's *Illustrations to Lord Byron's Life and Works* (1834) and *Illustrations of the Waverley Novels* (1833) are examples. It is sometimes possible to find old volumes of this kind with the prints still in good condition. They contain landscapes and portraits of well-known contemporary writers or fictional characters, which look most attractive when mounted in black and gold frames.

Prints and water colours often suffer from what is known as 'foxing', the name given to the brown spots or patches which often develop when they have at some time suffered from damp. These marks are not easily removed without damage to the picture. Expert treatment can be expensive and is probably merited only if a print is rare or has special value for the owner. When hanging prints and water colours see that the frame does not rest against the wall if there is the slightest possibility that it may at any time suffer from dampness. This can be done by sticking small pads of cork or rubber behind the lower corners of the frame.

Prints normally carry a good deal of interesting and useful information. On no account cut this away, or any other portion of a print, and do not buy prints which have been framed down to the edges of the picture, because this almost certainly means that the border with the title of the picture and the names of the artist and engraver have been removed. In fact, the cut-away portion can sometimes be seen pasted on the back-board. Prints that have been cut have little value.

The name of the artist is usually seen at the bottom left-hand corner of the print. If an engraving has been based on a painting, the name will be followed by 'pinxit' (or some variant); if based on a drawing, by 'delin' or 'del'. The name of the engraver is usually on the right-hand side and his name will be followed by 'fecit' or 'sculp' (sometimes 'sculpsit'). Thus:

D. Teniers, pinxit   T. Major, sculp

beneath an engraving would mean that Thomas Major had made the engraving from a painting by David Teniers. A good deal of other information is often included on a print – usually a title, the name and address of the publisher and often the date when it was printed.

Old maps, framed and hung on the wall, are full of interest, particularly if they show a county or district you know well. It is fascinating to compare the settlements, roads and by-roads with those of the landscape you know today. Celebrated mapmakers were Christopher Saxton (sixteenth century), John Speed and John Ogilby (seventeenth century) and Hermann Moll (eighteenth century). Their original maps with contemporary colour are of considerable value, but there are many fakes and even more reproductions. The latter are easy to identify but

hand-coloured fakes which have been washed over with a
colouring agent to make them look old are not so easy to
recognize. The key to authenticity is the watermark.
Hold the map up to the light. Very early specimens will
often show a watermark of vertical lines a little less than
two inches apart. In seventeenth-century maps the lines
were closer and are crossed by many other lines to form a
close grid. There is often a coat-of-arms, monogram or
maker's name. Those who wish to delve into the subject
are advised to consult Raymond Lister's book on *How to
Identify Old Maps and Globes* (G. Bell & Sons).

The little portraits known as miniatures were originally
made to be worn on the person but in Victorian times
they were already being used for wall decoration. Miniatures were made from the sixteenth century onwards and
the earliest examples were painted on parchment or
specially treated paper. By the first decade of the eighteenth century ivory was being used, a material which
proved to be very suitable as a base for water colours.
Sometimes oil paint or enamel was used on a copper base.
Many colour reproductions have been framed to look like
miniatures but they are not difficult to recognize once
removed from behind the glass.

Prices of miniatures vary enormously. Those which
bear the signatures or monograms of the famous sev-
enteenth-and eighteenth-century miniaturists may be
worth several hundred pounds, particularly if the subject
is named. A miniature of the Duke of Wellington by
Henry P. Bone was recently sold at a London auction for
£320. On the other hand, an unsigned miniature of a
'lady' or a 'gentleman' may sell for between £10 and
£20.

Many people could not afford to have miniatures
painted and contented themselves with simpler and
cheaper silhouettes, profiles cut with a knife from black
paper and mounted on a white or coloured background of

card, vellum or ivory. Early examples were mounted in oval brass frames painted on plaster or glass and clearly in imitation of the more expensive miniatures, but later examples were framed in wood or *papier mâché* for wall decoration. The best silhouettes were made in the reign of George III.

Samplers are often used for wall decoration. They were originally specimen stitches or patterns embroidered on linen in coloured thread, but in the eighteenth century children were given samplers to make as a needlework exercise. They often embroidered the letters of the alphabet, a motto or a proverb, usually adding their name and often the date. Proud mothers framed them for all to see, and the more colourful ones still have a certain charm. More elaborate pictures embroidered by expert needlewomen, often in silk, were sometimes framed in gilt. These are more expensive than samplers which can often be bought very cheaply.

Porcelain or pottery plates are sometimes used for wall decoration, though some people frown on this practice. However, good quality transfer-printed ware or handpainted porcelain can look most attractive and is certainly preferable to poor-quality paintings.

Firearms

Weapons attract many collectors. The field is wide and highly specialized, embracing armour, uniforms, swords and firearms of all kinds. There are even those who assemble Nazi relics. The keen student should begin by reading some of the many books available. When a purchase has been made it will probably be mounted on a wall for all to see. Firearms are of particular interest and it may be useful to mention a few significant dates.

The first true gun (earlier types needed two men to fire them!) was the match-lock which was invented in the middle of the fifteenth century. The device which fired the gun consisted of an arm holding a glowing wick or 'match' which made contact with the flash pan when the trigger was pulled. Match-locks were used by Oliver Cromwell in the seventeenth century and in parts of the Middle East until relatively recent times. Few survive in Britain outside museums.

The wheel-lock was invented in 1510 and was used until the end of the seventeenth century. A circular piece of steel was wound up by clockwork, using a key. When the trigger was pressed the steel spun round against some iron pyrites which gave off a shower of sparks. These fell on the flash pan and fired the gun. The operation was not unlike that of a modern cigarette lighter. Wheel-lock guns are uncommon, and certainly outside the range of the average collector.

The flint-lock followed in the middle of the sixteenth century and was in common use for three hundred years. It was simpler and the principle was similar to that of the wheel-lock but in reverse. The cock of the gun held a flint and when the trigger was pulled this flint struck a steel, showered sparks into the flash pan and fired the gun.

The percussion firearm was invented, oddly enough, by a Scottish minister, Alexander John Forsyth, who took out a patent in 1807. A detonating compound was struck by a hammer and the resulting flash fired the gun. By about 1830 it was generally agreed that percussion guns were less liable to misfire than the flint-lock and many flint-lock guns were converted into percussion weapons.

In 1830 the 'Pepper-box' was invented, a short gun with a rotating barrel using the percussion-cap principle. This was the first 'revolver.'

In 1840 there were two significant innovations – John Deringer perfected a small percussion pistol in America, and Samuel Colt invented a revolver which was eventually produced in large numbers. Colts bear serial numbers and early specimens with low numbers are now very valuable.

By the middle of the nineteenth century craftsmanship in gun-making was declining, but the early percussion firearms are often extremely beautiful and this is one reason why they are collected. Many bear silver mounts and it is sometimes assumed that the silver hallmark dates the gun. This may not be so since the mounts were made in quantity by silversmiths who supplied them in bulk to the gunmakers.

All firearms should bear what are known as proofmarks on the barrel. These show that the barrel has been tested for strength: in the early seventeenth century, before this was done, barrels were liable to shatter. The proofmarks, which changed from time to time, help the collector to date a gun. The only official Proof House in this country was at the Tower of London until 1813. After that date, guns could be officially marked at Birmingham.

As with most antiques, weapons in fine condition and which have been little used, especially if they are still in their original cases, are much sought after. When buying firearms, always check very carefully to make sure there are no replacement parts, particularly in the firing mechanisms since these often broke under the strain of use. Many flint-lock weapons which were converted to percussion between 1830 and 1850 have now been re-converted to flint-locks using old parts, simply for sale as antiques.

Before buying or selling *any* weapon it is important to know the regulations governing ownership. A firearms certificate is usually necessary for anyone who is in possession of a firearm, other than a smooth-bore gun with a barrel not less than twenty inches in length, or an air weapon. The word 'firearm' means any lethal, barrelled weapon of any description from which any shot, bullet or other missile can be discharged.

Book Collecting

Many rooms have fitted bookshelves or glazed bookcases and most people will prefer them to contain books which are of interest or value. Rows of books with fine old leather bindings may look very attractive but it is surely a mistake to keep books solely to look at. There is something rather depressing about a 'Wanted' advertisement which reads: 'Bindings for library furnishings, long or short sets, or single volumes in calf or morocco, nice appearance, sound condition first importance, full or half bound, gilt backs, contents immaterial'. Thousands of books of this type are sold every year solely for 'library furnishing'. Far better to fill your shelves with books for use, books of interest and books which in years to come may be of value to scholars and historians.

Why do people collect 'First Editions'? Some are valued largely because they are rare, like the work of the early makers of porcelain or silver. The more popular an author the less valuable first editions are likely to be. The novels of Dickens, for example, were published in first editions of up to 40,000 and unless you have good copies of the original serial parts, a bound first edition of Dickens will seldom fetch more than a few pounds. But some first editions are both rare and valuable. They are important to the scholar because it is important to know what the author intended people to read. As an ordinary booklover, you can share with the author's first readers the experience of reading his words as they first appeared in print. Later editions may well have been printed with omissions, or changes of which he may not have approved. Books which have been signed by the author and given to his friends, or which carry the signature of another eminent person, have added interest and value.

Books can be things of real beauty and great artistry can go into their production. Individual books of the kind which are the product of the crafts of printing and bookbinding are well worth having on the shelves. Look also for nineteenth-century books with illustrations by well-known artists.

It is easy for the beginner to assume that all old books must be worth something. This is by no means the case. The vast majority of old Bibles and books on religious subjects have little monetary value with, of course, a few notable exceptions. Certain Bibles and other odd books have what are known as fore-edge paintings. If you fan out the leaves of a book so that the edges of the pages are inclined at an angle of say forty-five degrees to the cover and fix it in that position, it is possible to draw or paint on the edges of the pages so that the design will not be seen when the book is closed, particularly if the edges are later gilded. This was fore-edge painting. Artists were employed in the seventeenth and eighteenth centuries to paint fore-edge designs, often to fulfil the same purpose as a book-plate – to identify the owner of the book. Fore-edge painting later became a hobby for young gentle-women.

When buying books, check carefully that nothing is missing. Engravings and maps may well have been removed by a previous owner for framing. The absence of an illustration, a single page or even a fly-leaf reduces the value.

Quite apart from antique books, it is perhaps worth mentioning here that the dust-wrappers on good modern books should not be removed. They protect the cover from fading and books with dust-wrappers are more valuable if you or your descendants ever wish to dispose of them.

THE CARE OF PICTURES

Oil paintings may need to be cleaned but never try to do so yourself: it is a job for an expert. Surface dirt accumulated over the years can, however, be carefully removed at home. A soft face cloth dipped in tepid, soapy water and wrung out can be used to wipe a varnished picture very gently. This will remove a great deal of the ingrained dirt without damage, though no water should be allowed to seep through to the canvas as damp may cause the oil paint to rise.

Pictures should never be hung above radiators and it is unwise to hang ivory miniatures on the chimney breast, a favourite place for these small portraits. The heat from a radiator or fire is liable to crack the ivory.

It is often said that gilt picture frames can be cleaned by careful application of a solution of bicarbonate of soda (one teaspoonful to a pint of water), but we have never succeeded in using this method without some slight damage to the gilt, which tends to rub off its plaster ground if any pressure is applied during the process.

The method recommended in *The Young Housewife's Daily Assistant* is gentler.

A gill of good vinegar in a pint of cold water, a *large* camel's hair brush (a shaving brush will do), and clean soft cloths. The frame must be perfectly free from dust. Dip the brush into the liquid, and squeeze it slightly, that it may not be too wet; brush the gilding (a small piece at a time) lightly, up and down, till it is quite restored. The brush must be constantly washed; and in finishing it should be squeezed dry, and the gilding brushed till dry.

One thing is certain, 'gold paint' should never be used on gilt frames.

CHAPTER ELEVEN

SMALL ORNAMENTAL ANTIQUES

THERE are many small decorative objects which look well on a side table or on the shelves of an alcove, and antique jewellery can be most attractive to wear. In this chapter, we mention a few items which may be bought reasonably today.

Buttons

Buttons for fastening clothes and for decorative purposes have been made over the years from a fantastic variety of materials – wood, bone, horn, ivory, tortoiseshell, glass, china, mother-of-pearl, *papier mâché*, silver, Sheffield plate, brass, enamel and so on. During the seventeenth and eighteenth centuries some very fine designers were employed, especially in France, to produce attractive types. Look for buttons made of Sheffield plate with heraldic designs, for mother-of-pearl buttons with incised designs, and china buttons transfer printed; or you may prefer to specialize in military buttons. The field is enormous and once you start a collection you will find that they turn up in all kinds of places from the old drawer turned out by your grandmother to the rubbish tray in a junk shop. If you live in an old house, you may even dig them up in the garden.

Dolls

Today, our fashion houses display their creations at special shows using live models. During the eighteenth

and nineteenth centuries, before the days of modern
transport, the model was a doll used as a traveller's
sample and when their primary purpose had been
fulfilled these dolls became playthings for children. In
early Victorian times, of course, dolls were also
specifically manufactured as toys and often took the form
of babies or small children. Many of these were made so
that the eyes would open and shut by pulling a wire. It
was much later, in the 1870s, that a lead weight was used
which caused the eyes to shut automatically when the
doll was laid down.

A dressed doll usually wore little shoes and stockings,
and often gloves, so that the only part of the body visible
would be the face and much care and attention was given
to making this realistic. Although all kinds of materials
were used for doll-making, wax and china provided the
greatest opportunities for artistry (see Illus. 28). The
name of Montain is particularly associated with the modelling of beautiful wax dolls, and Jumeau with the use of
unglazed or 'bisque' porcelain dolls.

The costumes, when original, usually help to determine
the date when a doll was made but there are one or two
useful pointers in their construction. Early dolls of the
eighteenth and early nineteenth centuries usually had
brown eyes. In Victorian times, the colour changed to
blue in honour of the Queen. Parian ware was used
for doll-making in the middle of the nineteenth century
and the white material evidently suggested a Nordic
type, for it is usually associated with fair hair. Dolls
made of *papier mâché* date from the early nineteenth
century.

Painted Enamels

The small enamel objects made at the Battersea and
South Staffordshire factories in the eighteenth and early

nineteenth centuries often show superb artistry. Little boxes to be carried in the pocket or *étui*, in which ladies kept small articles such as scissors, bodkins and snuff spoons, were produced in large numbers. They were made of copper to which was fused a thin layer of opaque coloured glass. The surface was then usually decorated with painted panels or with transfer work. The edges of most of the early examples were finished with a small strip of gilded metal. So precise was the workmanship that the lids of the boxes closed snugly, obviating the need for a catch.

Factories in South Staffordshire at Bilston and Wednesbury probably started production in the early 1750s and were still operating in the early nineteenth century. The Battersea factory, however, was a financial failure. It started in 1753 and was forced to close down three years later.

It is difficult even for the expert to distinguish between the Battersea enamels and those from South Staffordshire: there is no sure method of deciding which was made where. Colours are said to differ slightly, though even this is a matter of opinion. However, since there is little difference between the quality or current value of the work produced at any of the factories this is relatively unimportant.

When buying enamel work it is as well to remember that the surface, though hard, chips and cracks very easily. Many pieces have been damaged and repaired with paint. When this has just been done it is difficult to detect, but as time passes the paint discolours, making the repair work more obvious.

Small enamel boxes inscribed with mottoes or the name of a resort are quite common. Many have a mirror inside the lid. These boxes were produced in their thousands for the tourist trade during the nineteenth century. They are now being collected and, for their size and often indifferent quality, are commanding quite high prices, often between £20 and £30.

Both the Battersea and South Staffordshire factories produced limited numbers of larger pieces such as kettles, candlesticks, knife boxes, etc. These are comparatively rare and therefore valuable.

The Samson factory in Paris, which has copied old porcelain of many kinds, also copied enamel work, and many fakes were imported from Europe during the nineteenth century.

It is worth mentioning one or two other types of enamel which can be seen in some of our larger museums. *Cloisonné* enamel has already been described.

Champlevé enamel is the reverse of *cloisonné*. Instead of building up cells to hold the enamel on the surface, the metal body was carved to provide the design and the incised depressions were filled with coloured enamels. The surface was then polished. *Champlevé* enamels date from as early as the ninth and tenth centuries and the early work is very rare.

Limoges enamel is named after the French town where it was made over a very long period of time, especially during the sixteenth and seventeenth centuries. As with the Battersea and South Staffordshire work, the enamels were painted on a copper base. The early work is superb. It was copied profusely during the nineteenth century.

Jewellery

This is a wide and very specialized field which the amateur should study carefully before buying, unless an experienced friend is at hand to give advice.

Early jewellery, made before the eighteenth century, is rare but it does occasionally turn up in small shops and is often unrecognized. Quite recently, a seventeenth-century Spanish pendant with large rose-cut diamonds set in

filigree gold was sold for £12 by a dealer who thought
that the crude workmanship and irregularities of the
stones meant that it was a piece of little value. In fact, it
was worth well over £100. As with many such pieces, the
diamonds were greyish-brown in colour and the setting
was fashioned by hand in a carefree way. This mistake
was simply due to lack of knowledge and experience:
early Spanish jewellery has a distinctive style which, once
seen, is never forgotten.

We can do no more, however, than give a little basic
information about jewellery. First, remember that there
are three common qualities or standards of gold – 9 carat,
18 carat and 22 carat (pure gold is 24 carat). The value of
any piece which has gold in its make-up depends very
much on the carat standard. Gold is measured in penny-
weights of which there are twenty to the ounce. The
value of gold varies daily with world markets but it is
usually about £5 for a 9-carat ounce, £10 for an
18-carat ounce and £13 for a 22-carat ounce. Although colour can give some idea of the quality of gold –
9-carat gold is often yellower than the reddish, 22-carat
gold – it must be remembered that gold can be found in
colours and tones ranging from green to white. These
colours are sometimes used by goldsmiths to decorate
pieces with flowers or geometrical designs.

Most gold jewellery is stamped with the carat value,
together with a hallmark, but if this is missing a jeweller
can rub the gold on a porous black stone known as a
touchstone, dab the mark on the stone with acid, and
determine the purity of the gold by the effect the acid has
on the mark. But let us issue a warning here: we have
come across several brass pieces, notably watch-chains,
stamped with a 9-carat mark. All objects thought to be
gold should be tested with nitric acid, which has no action
whatsoever on gold. The object to be tested should be
filed in an inconspicuous place in order to remove a sur-

face layer of gold should the object be plated. If the acid turns green then the gold plate is on copper or brass: if it turns grey it is on silver.

When buying Alberts (nineteenth-century gold watch-chains) which have been made into charm bracelets, remember to check the links for wear where they rub together. At the same time, check the rings and padlock at the ends for hallmarks; unscrupulous dealers sometimes put cheap, plated ones on hallmarked chains. Among the most sought-after charms for bracelets are the gold-mounted seals which were often attached to old watch-chains.

Victorian jewellery was, on the whole, bold, imaginative and very well made. There was also a great deal of it, which is all to the good since it is at present very fashionable. Though gold seems to have been used without stint, the cost was kept down by the skilful use of semi-precious stones and seed pearls. However, before buying, it is as well to remember that 'all is not gold that glitters' for the Victorian jeweller was very fond of using an alloy of copper and zinc called 'Pinchbeck' (invented by a London watchmaker of that name) which looks remarkably like gold. Most jewellery in which gold or silver was used can be dated from the hallmarks.

In many old rings the amateur may jump to the conclusion that the clear sparkling stones are diamonds: it is probably wise to assume that this is not the case. They will often turn out to be zircons, or white sapphires or paste – another name for ordinary glass. Remember that diamonds can only be positively valued in daylight because the value depends largely on the colour (ie, whether it is tinged in any way) and this cannot be determined under artificial light. Many of the cheaper precious stones have flaws – cracks or marks within the actual stone. Contrary to popular belief, diamonds are not the only stones which will scratch the surface of glass. In fact, many hard substances will scratch glass if sharp enough and applied with enough pressure.

Diamonds are valued in carats but this is a measurement of volume and not weight as in the case of gold: they increase rapidly in value as the volume increases. Large stones are rare and value is related to this rarity. Precious stones should be taken to a reputable jeweller or gemologist for accurate identification.

Lockets

Lockets are the small hinged ornaments, often shaped like a heart or a padlock, which held a wisp of the loved one's hair, or a tiny photograph. They were made in great numbers in the nineteenth century and particularly in late Victorian times. They are usually made of silver, brass or other metal, often inset with a semi-precious stone of some kind, or perhaps a cameo.

Glass Paperweights

Decorative glass paperweights are all of nineteenth-century date. They were first made in England between 1820 and 1840 and consisted of a clear glass bun into the base of which was set a bust or profile cast in relief in china clay. These profiles were usually of the king, but famous personalities of the day were also used. They are said to have been the work of apprentices in the glass factories, who made them in their spare time and sold them as curios to boost their poor pay. They were made at Bristol and Nailsea, in London and Stourbridge and Birmingham. Nailsea produced domes of green glass in which air bubbles were made to form flower-like shapes.

Until 1845, there was an excise tax on coloured glass. Its removal encouraged an expansion in the trade.

Weights were made by covering clear glass with several layers of coloured glass and then grinding parts of it away to end with a panel of clear glass surrounded by a border of coloured stripes.

At this time (1845), the St Louis glassworks in Paris started to make the superb *millefiori* (thousand flowers) paperweights. These were buns of clear glass into the base of which were inserted canes of coloured glass. Each cane was made in a different shape and colour and contained pictures of animals or designs or letters. The design ran right through the canes like the lettering in a stick of rock. The most famous of these paperweights were made at the Clichy and Baccarat factories. Some have the initial of the factory and the date running through the canes. A few rarer weights contain glass insects, reptiles or flowers. Some weights produced at Stourbridge are very similar in style to the French types.

In most weights, the pontil mark has been ground out deep enough to reveal the lower end of the canes: on others the bottom has been ground flat and then cut with a multi-pointed star.

Good quality paperweights are now quite rare and command high prices. King Farouk, who was a great collector, was probably partly responsible for their rapid appreciation.

Buyers should beware of the many imitations. Thousands are at present being imported from Japan. Beware also of weights which have been chipped and subsequently ground and repolished. These usually appear to be rather small for the size of the decoration they contain.

Tea Caddies and Workboxes

'Britain is a nation of tea-drinkers.' How true this is and has been for a very long time. During the eighteenth century, tea-drinking was a social ritual and a great deal of money was spent on silver kettles and teapots. 'Taking tea' provided an opportunity for assessing the social standing of one's hosts. It is easy to see, therefore, why so much trouble was taken over the appearance of a tea caddy. They were made in a great variety of materials, including silver. Most were made of veneered or inlaid wood or of *papier mâché*: some were covered or inlaid with ivory or tortoiseshell. Most early caddies were fitted with locks to prevent pilfering by members of the household staff. After all, tea was expensive: in 1714 the cheapest tea, 'Bohea', cost from 9*s* to 25*s* a pound: 'Pekoe' was 45*s* a pound and green tea 16*s* a pound. Prices dropped a little during the 1720s and 1730s but by 1750 they were up again. During the Regency period mahogany, rosewood and walnut were used to make caddies in the shape of a sarcophagus. The majority of these later caddies had at least two compartments, one for green tea and one for black, and many had a mixing bowl for blending the teas to suit a personal taste.

Tea caddies supported on a pillar and taking on the role of a piece of furniture were an early nineteenth-century development and are known as 'teapoys', a name often used to describe the small mid-eighteenth century three-legged table from which tea was served.

Tea caddies cover a vast range of shapes and sizes and are decorative and useful things to have in the home.

Workboxes tended to be larger and more cumbersome than tea caddies. During the eighteenth and early nineteenth centuries, when needlework was a common pastime for ladies of leisure, they were used for keeping the silks, wools, needles and thimbles needed for tapestry and embroidery work. Most were made of wood and were lined inside with coloured paper or cloth. A padded pincushion usually occupied a prominent place and the rest of the box was divided into trays and receptacles for scissors, buttons, hooks and ribbons. Many of the accessories were made of ivory or boxwood and rather conspicuous 'secret' drawers were often included. These were sometimes padded and may have been intended for jewellery. As with tea caddies, workboxes were sometimes built as pieces of furniture supported on various types of pillar or leg, often with a cloth bag slung underneath to take wools. These were known as work tables. Many collectors get a great deal of pleasure from the search for antique needlework accessories with which to furnish an old workbox.

Snuff Boxes and Vinaigrettes

During the eighteenth and early nineteenth centuries, snuff-taking was a popular habit indulged in by both sexes, though the ladies were more secretive about it. Craftsmen recognized the need to produce small, decorative boxes with tight-fitting lids in which the snuff could be carried. The decoration of these boxes allowed the artist great freedom and the range is vast. Many people collect snuff boxes and they are commonly used for carrying pills. Gold and silver examples are most sought after and are very expensive when the actual weight of precious metal is considered.

Similar in many ways to the snuff box was the vinaigrette. These were small boxes of various shapes, sizes and decoration. They were usually of gold or silver and can be distinguished from the snuff box by the secondary pierced and hinged lid fitted inside. Beneath this grill was placed a small sponge soaked in aromatic vinegar. When the smells from candles, inadequate sewage disposal or unwashed clothing heavy with body odours became too much to stand, the box was opened and a 'whiff' was taken of the sweet-smelling vinegar. The grills of these boxes were often beautiful, chased with scrolls and flowers, etc. The silver vinaigrettes were always gilded inside to prevent the acid vinegar reacting with the silver. Vinaigrettes are as popular with collectors as snuff boxes.

Silver Buckles

These are usually Continental, most frequently Dutch. They have intricate moulded designs and there is always a ready market for them as there is a tradition among nurses always to wear a silver buckle on their uniform belts when they are qualified.

Thimbles

Thimbles are ideal for the collector with relatively little space for they can be displayed on tiny shelves no more than an inch wide. They are to be found in metal, silver, ivory, tortoiseshell and porcelain and many of them, even in Victorian times, were very beautiful – the metal ones chased, the porcelain ones painted.

CHAPTER TWELVE

SUGGESTIONS FOR THE NEW COLLECTOR

ONE of the most frequent questions asked of any person with an interest in antiques is: 'I would like to begin collecting. How do I start?' The answer depends very much on the amount of money the enthusiast has available and the reasons behind this urge to collect. Some want to invest capital; others want to collect and furnish at the same time; and there are those who want to do it for the fun they hope to get out of it. The would-be investor should consult a reputable dealer. Those who want to furnish should decide on a style and a maximum expenditure and then keep looking until they find the things they want at a price they can pay. This chapter is addressed to those who want to start collecting as a hobby and who have little money to spare.

The first and obvious fact is that anything that is generally regarded as beautiful or rare will be too expensive: the sights must be set lower. Here are a few suggestions:

Porcelain

Collections of porcelain made by well-known factories can be acquired quite cheaply if you are prepared to accept slightly damaged pieces. The accumulation of representative specimens from the different factories makes it possible to handle the pieces, to distinguish between them and between the genuine and the fake. A collection of odd cups and saucers from the famous eighteenth-century factories can be made without spending a great deal of money. They look attractive when displayed in a cabinet and can occasionally be married.

Drinking Glasses

Odd eighteenth-century glasses constantly crop up in junk shops and in job lots at salerooms. They can usually be bought quite cheaply. There is a vast range of shapes and sizes but, nevertheless, they can look very attractive when set out on a tray and, once again, there is always the chance of making up a set. The great thing about collecting glasses is that they can be used, but don't be tempted to buy damaged glasses: these can be both dangerous and unhygienic.

Silver Spoons

Attractive representative collections can be made of odd silver spoons. Aim at finding one of each style and period from George I onwards. The size of the spoons will depend on the size of your wallet.

Oriental Blue and White

Porcelain decorated with underglaze blue and made for export from China during the nineteenth century, often referred to as Nankin ware after the port from which it was shipped, can be seen in most antique shops. It has so far been rather frowned on by collectors because it does not reach the high quality of eighteenth-century work. However, it is slowly gaining in favour, is still within the range of the average collector, and is very decorative.

Commemorative Medals and Small Plaques

These often seem to hang around antique shops for ever because there are relatively few serious collectors of these medals. They can be bought for a few shillings each, since they are usually made of bronze or brass. Silver ones, of course, are more expensive because of their scrap value. This is a wide field for collectors because any occasion of note in the late eighteenth century and during the nineteenth century, both here and overseas, seems to have had a plaque or medal struck to commemorate the event.

Silk Pictures

The city of Coventry has always been noted for the weaving of silk ribbon: in the first half of the nineteenth century it was the chief occupation of its people. Then, about 1860, came a serious slump in the ribbon trade and unemployment became so acute that several thousand people left the city to look for work elsewhere. At this time a certain young man, Thomas Stevens, who by hard work and inventiveness had already acquired his own business, had been experimenting on his looms, trying to produce pictures in silk. The slump gave him his opportunity. He successfully turned out all manner of small decorative ribbon articles which could carry his pictures – birthday and Christmas 'cards', Valentines, bookmarks, scent sachets, badges and hat ribbons; by 1880, his woven silk pictures were being mounted and framed as pictures. During the phenomenal expansion of his business a new factory had been built, the Stevengraph Works, and the term Stevengraph is now the name given to these Coventry silk pictures.

Great interest has recently been shown in the articles made by Thomas Stevens and a Stevengraph Collectors' Association has been formed in America. The prices paid for Stevengraphs have risen steeply, particularly of those relating to America. A specimen showing the signing of the Declaration of Independence recently fetched over £120 at auction. We mention them briefly here so that if

you come across a Stevengraph between the pages of an
old book, among old letters, or when clearing out a
drawer, you will recognize it for what it is and know that
it has value.

Art Nouveau

Although it is not antique, *art nouveau* decoration has
been accepted in the fashionable world and has recently
come into the limelight. It followed the work of people
such as William Morris and Burne Jones and continued
from the 1890s into the early years of the present century.

In Britain, the best known names are those of Aubrey
Beardsley, the artist, and Rennie Mackintosh, the Scottish designer. A well-known firm of London auctioneers
has recently held *art nouveau* sales, where it became
obvious that the things to collect are signed pieces by
artists of the *art nouveau* movement. These are more
plentiful than one might imagine. Look out for names
such as Gallé and Daum, the famous French glassmakers
of the period, and for the name of Tiffany, the big American store that sponsored so many artists of the movement and commissioned work from them.

Autographs

Many children and some adults keep an autograph album
and collect the signatures of the famous. It is an interesting hobby, though such single autographs are rarely of
much value. Signed letters or papers, however, are of
great interest, especially to biographers and scholars because they often throw light on the character of a person
and the events of his life. These often realize quite high
prices at auction. Such documents do turn up from time
to time among old family papers or even between the

pages of a book. Look out for them and treasure them.

Coins

The collection of coins has attracted great interest in recent years. Strangely enough many old coins – Roman coins, for example – seem to attract less attention than Victorian coins and often fetch lower prices.

The most important point to be noted by the prospective collector is the difference between the 'states' as they are called – 'mint', 'extra-fine', 'fine', etc. A coin in mint condition has not been touched since it was minted and cased. The mild acid constantly present on the skin is enough to mark the surface of coins when handled, a mark which only the very experienced collector will detect. Collectable coins should be treated with great care: scratches, dents or the rubbing of the edges reduce their value. Most of the really high prices are paid for commemorative sets of coins in their presentation cases.

Coin collecting has perhaps gained in popularity because of the detailed catalogues issued by the trade which give lists of coins with the prices paid for them in their several states.

Greetings Cards and Postcards

Valentines go back well over two centuries and became extremely popular in the nineteenth century. Christmas cards came in much later: the earliest recorded is dated 1843. Postcards were not in common use until 1870. All these are well worth collecting. Valentines were often produced on lace-like paper decorated with flowers and with charming verses, although there were also comic types designed to 'debunk' the sentimentality of early Victorian times.

Early postcards are a fascinating reflection of nine-teenth-century life and cover a vast field, pictorial, commemorative and humorous. There were also many 'novelty' postcards with feathers, hair and cloth glued to them, or cards which revealed another picture when held to the light. One great advantage of the postcard is that it can usually be roughly dated by the postmark.

One of the great thrills of collecting is the purchase of an article which intrigues you for reasons which you cannot really understand. The detective work and research involved slowly lead to an understanding of the article and, having solved your problem, you will hardly be able to wait before you get involved again. Many dealers who have given up the antique business because of its stresses and strains, continue to collect because they cannot live without the excitement of the chase. As they say in the trade: 'The big buy is just around the corner'. It could be yours tomorrow.

SOME USEFUL BOOKS

The books listed below are inexpensive, small and light enough to carry when travelling. A detailed bibliography of books about all classes of antiques can be found in *The Buying Antiques Reference Book* (David & Charles).

A Pocket Guide to the Marks of Origin on British and Irish Silver Plate (1544–1960) *and old Sheffield Plate Makers Marks* (1743–1860): Frederick Bradbury, (J. W. Northend, Sheffield)

Pocket Book of English Ceramic Marks: J. P. Cushion (Faber)

Antiques in their Periods: Hampden Gordon (Murray)

Antiques: The Amateur's Questions: Hampden Gordon (Murray)

Old English Furniture: A Simple Guide: Hampden Gordon (Murray)

'Country Life' Collectors' Pocket Book: G. Bernard Hughes

'Country Life' Pocket Book of China: G. Bernard Hughes

'Country Life' Pocket Book of Glass: Geoffrey Wills

GLOSSARY OF TERMS USED
IN THE ANTIQUE TRADE

Acanthus: A type of leaf decoration popular since the classical period and widely used on items made from wood or metal (see Illus. 13).

Andirons: Firedogs used to support lengths of burning wood on the hearth.

Apron: The box frame above the legs and beneath the top of a table or the seat of a chair.

Argyle: A spouted vessel, usually of silver or silver plate, in which gravy was kept hot by means of a liner filled with hot water. The name is said to be after a Duke of Argyll who was irritated when his gravy arrived at the dining table, which was some distance from the kitchen, with a skin of cool fat on the surface.

Armorial: The crest or coat-of-arms of a family or families was often engraved on silver, carved on wood, or painted on china belonging to that household. This is armorial ware. Armorial porcelain is particularly sought after by collectors.

Astragal: A convex moulding: a term used in furniture to describe the bars between the panes of a glazed bookcase or cabinet.

Atelier: A studio or workshop.

Bail Handle: A form consisting of a half-loop of metal secured by bolts; it was popular between 1720 and 1780.

Ball and Claw: A type of decoration usually used for feet or supports representing a lion's paw (or sometimes a bird's foot) with the claws extended over a ball. It is used on furniture, silver and occasionally on porcelain. It was much used during the eighteenth century and was favoured by Chippendale though it was not his original design (see Fig 6j).

Balloon Back: The shape of a chair back which resembles a partly-inflated balloon. It developed during the Victorian period (see Fig 5f).

Baluster: The bulbous, almost pear-shaped part of the stem of a drinking glass; the leg of a piece of furniture or any supporting column.

Banding: A decoration of the edges of a piece of furniture with a thin strip of veneer of a different colour and texture from the main body.

Baroque: A seventeenth-century style of decoration with extravagant curves and much foliage. It is often fussy, but full of life.

Bas Relief: Modelling on the surface of an article in low relief – ie, the modelling has very little depth.

Bentwood: Wood for making furniture which has been bent into shape in one piece by steam heating. Commonly found in Victorian rocking chairs.

Bergère: A French term used for a padded and up-holstered armchair. It is now used for English chairs made in the same French style and also for chairs with caned panels.

Bijouterie: A term for jewellery or trinkets, but sometimes used to describe a small display table on which the objects on view are protected by a glass-topped case.

'Billies and Charlies': Billy and Charlie were the names of two London workmen who made small leaden objects, mainly figures, with early dates impressed on them. They buried these objects in the ground on the site where they were digging and later dug them up again and sold them as genuine finds to eager unsuspecting

spectators who were watching their excavations. They are now much sought after by collectors.

Birdcage Table: A single-pillared table which has a small box at the top of the column the sides of which are formed of four vertical columns. The tabletop rests upon this and it enables the table to be both revolved and tipped.

Biscuit: The name given to pottery and porcelain when it has been fired in an unglazed state.

Bocage: A background of flowers or trees to porcelain or pottery figures.

Bombé: The shape of a piece of furniture which is bulbous, the lower part being the widest. French in origin.

Bonbonnière: A box or container for bonbons or sweets.

Bone China: A hard-paste porcelain containing bone ash which can be modelled thinly and still retain its strength. It is very translucent and has superseded most other types of porcelain in Britain.

Bonheur du jour: A ladies' writing table of delicate proportions.

Boulle or *Buhl:* A term used to describe a piece of furniture made in the style introduced by a seventeenth-century French furniture-maker of that name. He specialized in brass and tortoiseshell inlay work.

Bracket Foot: A foot formed from two shaped or square pieces of material – usually wood – mounted at right angles to form a bracket. This style of foot is used in place of a leg to raise the object above the surface on which it stands (see Fig 7m).

Breaker: A book which is to be broken up for the prints or maps it contains.

Breakfront: A term used to describe a piece of furniture in which the central portion either projects slightly forward or is recessed, breaking the main horizontal line set by the two ends. It is usually found in bookcases or in sideboards or dressers.

Britannia Metal: An alloy of antimony, copper and tin which was often silver-plated. It was first used in the eighteenth century and was popular during the Victorian period. It is cheap, very malleable, and has a dull ring when tapped.

Bunfoot: A bun-shaped foot commonly used during the William and Mary period and in much early oak furniture, particularly on chests (see Fig 7k).

Bureau-plat: A writing table.

Cabriole: The leg of a table or chair which curves first outward and then inward from the top to the base, tapering until it reaches the foot (see Fig 6b).

Cadogan Teapot: These teapots are usually made of brown-glazed earthenware with Chinese influence decoration in relief. They are lidless and have to be filled through a hole in the base and with tea that has already been strained.

Candle box: A small wooden box with a base extended lengthwise in one direction. A hole is cut in this extension to make it possible to hang the box on a wall. It is usually made of oak with a sliding top, and was used for storing candles.

Canapé: A sofa (French).

Canted: A term used to describe a bevelled corner.

Canterbury: A small piece of furniture, rather similar in design to a modern magazine rack, made for storing sheet music. They usually stand on short legs with castors and often have a carrying handle in the centre. Larger versions were made to store artists' portfolios of drawings. They were first made in the Georgian period and are much in demand today.

Canton: A port of southern China noted for the export of delicately coloured enamel or copper objects of all types. They were sent to Europe during the eighteenth

and nineteenth centuries. Much English porcelain was
sent to Canton to be decorated.

Carcase: The basic structure of a piece of furniture before
the finishing veneers and inlays are applied: it is
usually made of oak, deal or pine.

Card-cut: A term usually applied to a method of decorating silver and occasionally furniture. A flat piece of
silver with the edges cut in a decorative fashion is laid
on the surface of the main body, much as a decorative
hinge may be laid upon a door. It is commonly found
in early silver.

Carlton-House Table: A rather elegant D-shaped desk or
writing table with long rounded tapering legs and with
banks of drawers in a semicircle on the top at the back.
Carlton-House tables look severe and functional with
their undecorated clean lines. The design for these
tables was made for the Prince of Wales when he lived
at Carlton House.

Carolean: A term used to describe antiques made in the
reign of Charles I. The style persisted into the second
half of the seventeenth century.

Cartouche: Now a generally accepted term in the antique
trade for a decorated frame within which a coat-of-
arms, crest, or the initials or trade mark of a firm, are
carved, drawn or etched.

Carver: The name generally given to an open-armed
dining chair. There are usually two carvers to every six
ordinary dining chairs and they were used by the heads
of a household, who were usually responsible for carving the meat at dinner. It is sometimes said that the
name was derived from a chair used by Admiral
Carver.

Caryatid: A carved figure – usually female – used as a
support in furniture. The caryatid support derives from
Greek architecture.

Cassolette: A vessel or box for burning perfume.

Caster: A vessel originally used for shaking or dredging brown sugar over sweets. It resembles a large pepper pot and was made of silver or pewter.

Castor: The small wheel mounted on the legs of furniture to facilitate movement. Initially made of wood or leather, later of brass or porcelain.

Cat: A form of three-legged trivet or tripod usually made of wood but sometimes of brass or silver. Used for warming dishes in front of a fire.

Caudle Cup: A cup used for a mixture of spiced gruel and ale or wine.

Celadon: Chinese porcelain decorated with a pale jade-green translucent glaze.

Cellarette: A case for storing wine in the dining-room. They were usually placed beneath the sideboard.

Chafing Dish: Portable metal dish, often of silver, in which food could be kept warm.

Chaise-longue: A long couch usually with one end and a partial back normally used as an individual day bed.

Chalice: A cup or goblet usually associated with religious service.

Chamfered: A term describing the result of cutting away the wood which forms the edge between two flat surfaces to form a bevelled edge.

Champlevé: A method of decorating a metal object with enamels in which small cells are scooped out of the main body and filled with molten coloured enamels. This work is often found on French ecclesiastical items. It reached its peak of popularity at Champlevé in the fifteenth century.

Chapter Ring: A circular piece of metal on which the hours are marked on a clock or sundial. On older clocks they were usually of brass which had been silvered.

Charger: A large dish.

Chasing: Surface decoration on silver or other precious metal produced by hammering with a small blunt tool.

No cut is made and no metal removed.

Chatelaine: An attachment which could be clipped on a lady's belt. From it, a number of useful articles were suspended by a chain – scissors, an ivory notepad, pencil, case containing needles, button-hook, etc. Chatelaines were often made of silver.

Chevron: A zig-zag inlay or moulding.

Chiffonier: A small narrow sideboard, often with a shelf or shelves at the back and a cupboard beneath. The cupboard doors were often fitted with grille fronts backed with pleated, coloured silk. They were popular during the Regency and Victorian periods.

Chinoiserie: A term used to describe decoration which has been influenced by the popularity of Chinese art. It reached its height in England during the eighteenth century and is found in all materials.

Chocolate Pot: A large pot similar in shape to a coffee pot for serving hot chocolate, a popular drink during the early eighteenth century. Spouts on chocolate pots are usually placed high up on the body to try and avoid the risk of pouring out any thick residue which may have settled on the bottom. The knob of the pot can often be removed to allow a long thin spoon to be inserted for stirring.

Clapper or *Knocker*: A dealer who normally works without a shop, travelling around the country knocking on people's doors in the hope of buying any antiques they may be willing to part with. He normally sells these or he might even work for another dealer.

Clean Piece: Unrepaired and undamaged.

Cloisonné: A type of decoration made popular by the Chinese, in which wires were soldered to the body of a metal vessel (usually copper) to form a design. The decoration was then split up with more wires to form little cells which were filled with different coloured enamels. It was then fired and polished.

Coaster: A small, round dish, often of silver or Sheffield plate, with a turned wooden base on which decanters or bottles were stood. The base was covered with baize so that it would slide or 'coast' over a polished surface. These coasters were usually made in sets of four. More elaborate types were fitted with wheels so that they resembled small waggons.

Cock-beading: The thin strips of wood which fit around the front edge of a drawer.

Coffer: A chest.

Commode: A chest-of-drawers in the French style: or a chair, a small cupboard, or a small flight of steps for use in a bedroom, concealing a chamber pot.

Comport: A dish for fruit or sweets on a stand which raises it above table level.

Console Table: A small table with a single front leg which stands against and is given support by a wall. Console tables are often gilded.

Cooler: A small glass or porcelain bowl similar to a fingerbowl except that it has one or two small lips in which the stem of a drinking glass could rest while the bowl cooled.

Corner Chair: A chair with its legs so arranged and the back so shaped that it will stand in a corner.

Cornice: The projecting horizontal top of a piece of furniture.

Court Cupboard: An open-shelved oak cupboard of the Tudor period. These continued to be fashionable until the Commonwealth.

Crazing: A network of fine cracks in the glaze of porcelain or pottery.

Credence or *Credenza:* An Italian sideboard or serving table.

Cross-banding: A strip of decorative veneer chosen so that the grain of the wood runs in a different direction from the grain of the ground into which it is mounted.

Damascened: A piece of metal is said to have been damascened when other metals have been beaten into hollows in its surface. Steel armour was often damascened with gold and silver, especially in Milan during the sixteenth century. The process was first used in Damascus.

Dentil: A form of decorative moulding, usually found on the cornice of a piece of furniture. It consists of small rectangular shapes used in rows so that they resemble teeth.

Dolphin Foot: A decorative foot in which a dolphin's head becomes the base and the upturned tail the support. William Kent used this design between 1730 and 1740.

Dovetail: The fan-shaped joint most commonly seen where the front of a drawer is attached to the sides.

Dowel: A wooden pin used on most old oak furniture to secure joints. Dowels were used in preference to nails: their roughly circular heads can usually be clearly seen.

Dredger: See *Caster.*

Drop Handles: Brass handles resembling elongated drops of moisture. They were popular during the reign of William and Mary.

Drops: Pear-shaped pieces of cut glass hanging from a chandelier or glass ornament.

Duchesse: Two facing *bergère* chairs with a stool between them.

Dumb Waiter: A tall column or pillar supporting wooden trays of various sizes and levels. Dumb waiters were usually made of best quality mahogany. They were used to hold food and drink so that servants could be dispensed with during meals and also for more infor-

mal occasions to provide what we should now call a
'buffet' meal.

Embossed: Relief work on silver or copper. See
Repoussé.

Engine-turned: A term used to describe pottery that has
been decorated, before firing, on a lathe specially designed to produce the pattern. Small metal articles,
such as snuff boxes, were sometimes engine-turned.

Epergne: A multi-branched stand, usually of glass or
silver, or a combination of the two, though sometimes
of porcelain. Each branch terminated in a vase or dish
for flowers or sweetmeats. On some epergnes, there was
a large dish at the top of the stand for fruit. An epergne
usually stood in the centre of a dining table and is typi-
cally nineteenth century.

Escritoire: A writing cabinet on a stand or chest-of-
drawers. They were popular in the late eighteenth
century.

Escutcheon: A brass or ormolu plate which surrounds a
keyhole. The name derives from the shield-shaped
ground on which coats-of-arms are found.

Etui: A small decorative container, often of silver or
enamel, in which ladies kept items such as needles,
bodkins, toothpicks and snuff spoons.

Faience: A Continental tin-glazed earthenware, especially important in France during the eighteenth century. It was sometimes enamelled over the glaze and
this type of faience can be mistaken for porcelain.

Farthingale Chair: An armless chair with a tall, thin,
tapered back used by ladies wearing hooped petticoats
or farthingales.

Fauteuil: A French chair with unpadded arms similar in
design to the padded *bergère*. It may, however, have
padded elbows.

Festoon: Decoration formed by a carved, modelled or
painted garland of flowers, leaves or fruit, usually

bound with ribbons, suspended from the ends and hanging down in the middle. Articles with such decoration are said to be swagged.

Fine: A term used by the trade to describe high quality.

Finial: An ornamental projection such as the knob on a cover or the decorated apex of a pediment or canopy.

Flammiform: In the shape of a flame.

Fluting: A series of grooves cut or pressed into an article.

Foliate: Ornamented with leaves.

Foxing: The discoloration produced by the brown spots or patches which appear on paper that has been affected by damp.

Fretted: Carved in decorative patterns made up of straight lines.

Frieze: The horizontal band of wood beneath a cornice on furniture. Originally an architectural term.

Friggers: Articles made of glass more for diversion than for use. They were often designed to test the skill of the glassblower and included glass hats, pipes, walking sticks, rolling pins, etc.

Frit: A type of glass used by potters when glazing their wares.

Gadrooning: A form of decoration on the edges of furniture, silver and ceramics made up of convex curving lobes, or sometimes straight lobes.

Gallery: The term used for the vertical fencing around the top of furniture, trays, etc. These galleries are often fretted.

Gesso: A relief decoration modelled with a mixture of size and plaster or whiting over which gold leaf has been applied. It is found on furniture, mirrors and picture frames.

Gilding: Gold leaf applied to smooth surfaces – often to softwood coated with plaster of Paris – to enrich the decoration.

Gimmel: Two glass bottles fused together.

Girandole: A carved and gilded candle-holder for the wall, often with a mirror back plate.

Glaze: A translucent vitreous coating applied to porcelain and pottery which gives the finished articles a sheen. Different mineral substances in the glaze produce various colours in glazing.

Grisaille: Paintings which give a three-dimensional effect using only tones of one colour, usually grey.

Handcooler: A small egg-shaped object of glass or stone. It was held in a lady's hand to prevent perspiration on the palm.

Herringbone: A type of veneered decoration using a dark and light wood alternately in a series of small arrow-heads.

Hollands: The name used for gin from about 1770 to the 1840s. It derives from the Dutch *Hollandsch genever* (Holland gin).

Hood: The top portion of a long-case or grandfather clock which contains the glass. It will slide forward and off to make the working parts accessible.

Hoof Foot: A foot in the shape of an animal's hoof.

Horsehair: The hair from a horse's mane and tail used for covering or padding upholstered furniture because of its long-lasting resilience. It was sometimes woven to form a covering and was first used in the seventeenth century.

Impressed: An impressed mark is one applied with pressure.

Incised: Decoration cut into the surface of the body.

Inlay: Pictures and decorative motifs, made up of woods of various colours, set into the actual body of a piece of furniture. Bone, ivory, tortoiseshell, mother-of-pearl and brass were also sometimes used in inlay work.

Intaglio: An incised engraving in a hard surface.

Ironstone: A form of pottery with a very hard glassy

body, obtained by adding furnace slag to the clay of which it was made.

Japanning: A lacquer finish which is very hard, usually applied to softwood and to *papier mâché*, iron and tin articles. It is most often seen in red or black. The process originated in Japan.

Jardinière: A classical vase-shaped container or stand used for plants or flowers. *Jardinières* vary greatly in size.

Joynt: Catalogues sometimes refer to a joynt stool. This means a jointed piece in which mortice and tenon joints are secured with dowel pins.

Kaolin: The name given to the white hard-paste china clay dug in Devon and Cornwall and first used in England by William Cookworthy.

Key Pattern: A design of straight lines joining at right angles (Illus. 14) used to decorate borders, especially of furniture and silver.

Knee: The outward curving part of a leg which marks the change of direction from the near horizontal towards the near vertical.

Knocker: See *Clapper.*

Knife Box: A container in which knives were kept, usually on a sideboard. Knife boxes were sometimes incorporated in designs of sideboards, particularly those of the Adam style.

Knocked Down: Sold at auction.

Knock-out: A term used for a private auction which may take place among dealers after they have completed their transactions in an ordinary saleroom.

Knop: A decorative knob or finial to a lid, or a shaped enlargement included in the stem of a glass which may take many forms, eg, an acorn, a ball, a cushion.

Knurled: Scrolled. A term applied to the foot of a chair or table (see Fig 6i).

Lacquer: A coating of the sap of the lac tree applied by

dissolving shellac in alcohol which evaporates, leaving a thin layer on the lacquered article. See *Japanning*.

Ladder Back: The back of a chair with several bracing struts which run horizontally like the rungs of a ladder.

Library Chair: A chair popular during the eighteenth century which could be sat on or astride. It had a book-rest which could be raised on a ratchet at the back. The arms often contained hinged compartments for ink, pens, etc. The chair was bestridden for reading or writing.

Library Steps: Elegant flights of steps which enabled the user to reach books from high shelves. The tread of the steps could often be raised revealing useful storage space. Much ingenuity was used by cabinet-makers to design library steps which would fold to form a chair or a table.

Limoges Enamel Ware: Copper articles decorated with coloured enamels, usually black, white or terracotta, and depicting classical legends. The finest Limoges enamel was produced in the sixteenth century: it was much copied in the nineteenth century.

Liner: The vessel, often of dark blue glass, which is placed inside a silver or plated salt cellar to hold the salt.

Lion's Mask: The lion's head was ideal as a design for decorative handles often with a ring hanging from the nose. It was widely used on silver and furniture, especially during the eighteenth century and during the Regency period. It is also seen on porcelain.

Lithograph: A reproduction of a picture or drawing taken from a limestone block.

Lithophane: A small plaque of white or cream porcelain into which a picture is moulded in relief giving varying degrees of translucency. In Victorian times, they were placed in front of candles which gave the picture depth when seen from the front.

Loper: The vertical slide which is drawn out on either side of a fall-front bureau or desk to support the writing surface.

Lot: An article or group of articles to be sold at auction for a single sum of money.

Love Seat: An upholstered couch for two people.

Loving Cup: A two-handled mug or goblet.

Lowboy: A low chest-of-drawers. Originally an American term.

Lustre: A vase from the top rim of which are suspended a number of cut-glass drops which catch the light. They were usually made in pairs.

Lustre Decoration: A thin film of metal on pottery or porcelain.

Lyre: A shape derived from the musical instrument of that name. It was popular during the French Empire and Regency periods for the backs of chairs, ends of tables, etc.

Majolica: Italian tin-glazed earthenware decorated with brightly coloured enamel and dating from the sixteenth century. Imitation majolica was also made by English factories in the second half of the nineteenth century.

Marbling: Decoration intended to produce a variegated pattern like marble.

Marquetry: Decorative motifs covering the surface of a piece of furniture made up of veneers of various colours and contrasting grains inlaid in the darker veneered background.

Marrow Spoon or Marrow Scoop: A silver or plated spoon with a long shallow bowl, often double-ended, used for scraping the marrow from bones.

Mazarine: A pierced straining dish used for serving boiled fish from the early eighteenth century onwards. The name is derived from Jules Mazarin, Cardinal of France, and a connoisseur.

Medallion: A panel, usually round or oval in shape, used for decoration.

Millefiori: A decoration normally found at the base of paperweights. The floral appearance is created by a series of coloured glass rods cut off to leave the exposed ends uppermost encased in a clear glass bun.

Monteith: A punch bowl. Silver examples often have a detachable upper rim which is notched or scalloped. The notches supported the bases of wine glasses while the bowls were cooled in the iced water inside the Monteith.

Mote-skimmer: A long thin teaspoon, often of silver, the bowl of which is pierced with holes, the end of the handle terminating in a barb. The bowl was used to remove leaves from a cup of tea; the barb was used to clean the strainer in the teapot.

Mother-of-pearl: The nacreous iridescent lining from a sea-shell.

Nailer: A term used by clappers or dealers for an object which first excites curiosity or greed of a buyer or seller. For the buyer, it is often a quality antique displayed among poorer quality items in the shop window of an unscrupulous dealer. It is usually unpriced and not for sale. For the seller, it is usually a valueless item on which the unscrupulous dealer places a high value with no intention of buying, in the hope that the seller will be so impressed that he will be willing to sell other and better items at low prices.

Nosing: A casing, usually of brass, at the base of a table leg to which the castor is attached.

Nutmeg Grater: A metal plate similar to a modern kitchen grater usually contained in a decorative mount. The larger ones were in carved ivory, the portable ones in silver or gold boxes.

Ogee Foot: A bracket foot with a double curve (convex above and concave below) commonly used from the time of George II (see Fig 7).

Opaline: A translucent glass, usually white, that shows a fiery-red glow when seen against a strong light.

Ormolu: Decoration cast in brass or bronze and gilded.

'Over the Odds': Above current market value.

Oviform: Egg-shaped.

Oyster Veneer: A veneer selected for its grain, which resembles the concentric rings on an oyster shell.

Pap-boat: An oval-shaped vessel with a small lip or spout for feeding babies. In the early eighteenth century they were made of silver but they can also be found in porcelain or pottery.

Papier Mâché: A term used for articles made from layers of pulped paper soaked in a mixture of chalk or flour and glue compressed into shape, and heated. Nearly all *papier mâché* articles are finished with black lacquer and decorated.

Parcel Gilt: This term, often used in the trade, is the old English way of saying partly gilt or partly gilded.

Parian Ware: A soapy white unglazed porcelain used for making figures and busts.

Parquetry: A mosaic of geometrical pieces of wood fitted together as a veneer on furniture. Today, we use the word 'parquet' to describe a wood-block floor.

Paste: The clay or mixture of which a piece of porcelain or pottery is made.

Paste Jewellery: Jewellery in which glass is used in imitation of precious stones.

Pastille Burners: Small decorative pottery and porcelain ornaments, often in the form of houses or cottages. They have an aperture in the back into which a small pastille was placed. When ignited, this gave off a perfumed vapour.

Pâte-sur-Pâte: A method of decorating porcelain using thin white translucent slip on a coloured ground. It was introduced by Mark Louis Solon when he came over from France in 1870 to work at the Minton factory. It originated in the Sèvres factory.

Patera: A small decorative disc used on furniture especially during the Adam period.

Patina: The surface condition acquired by wood or metal through years of polishing and normal household use.

Pediment: An architectural term used for the triangular gable-end of a building with a low-pitched roof. In furniture it is a triangular-shaped addition to a cornice of a bookcase, cabinet or clock.

Pestle and Mortar: The mortar is a brass, bronze or stoneware bowl; the pestle is a short, heavy, round-ended rod usually of the same material used to powder or pulverize materials – usually drugs – in the mortar.

Pewter: An alloy of tin with lead, copper or antimony.

Pie-crust: A method of decorating the edge of an object with carved concave depressions so that it resembles a pie-crust after it has been thumbed.

Pinchbeck: This is often known as 'Poor man's gold'. It was an alloy of which the basic metal was brass invented by Christopher Pinchbeck, a clockmaker. The alloy looks very like gold and does not tarnish quickly: it was used a great deal in making Victorian jewellery.

Plaque: An ornamental tablet of metal or china used to decorate furniture.

Pontil Mark: The point at which a glass article is snapped from the pontil or punty – the iron rod on which it was worked. In most old glass this shows as a sharp and jagged surface. In later glass the pontil mark was ground off or sometimes covered with a blob of molten glass.

Porringer: A double-handled bowl used for porridge. Porringers were popular during the seventeenth and early eighteenth centuries.

Posset: This was a drink made from hot milk curdled

with ale or wine, and was often spiced. It was taken as a remedy for colds and drunk from posset pots or posset cups which were often lidded.

Posy Holder: A cone-shaped vase, often of silver, into which a posy could be inserted without water. A pin which was attached to the holder by a chain could be pushed through a hole in the holder and out the other side to hold the posy in place. The posy holder itself was often attached in some way to the wearer.

Potato Ring: A circular, pierced silver ring, usually three to four inches high, which was used on a dining table to support a dish of hot potatoes and so prevent damage to the polished surface beneath. Another school of thought believes that they were placed on wooden platters with the hot potatoes inside. They were commonly made and used in Ireland in the second half of the eighteenth century.

Pot Pourri: A mixture of dried petals, herbs or spices kept in a container for its perfume. The name is often used for the actual container – a pottery or porcelain jar, for example.

Pricket: The spike on the sconce of old candlesticks which was driven into the base of the wax candle to support it.

Printies: Concave cuts, round or oval in shape, used to decorate glass vessels, especially decanters.

Privates: A term used by dealers for private individuals with no trade connexions who bid at sales.

Prunt: A small blob of molten glass, often decorated to resemble a raspberry, applied to the main body of a glass article, as decoration. They were occasionally used to hide the pontil mark.

Puffer: The trade term for a person at an auction sale, in league with an unscrupulous auctioneer, who bids against a genuine buyer in order to run the price up.

Punter: A purchaser who is prepared to take a chance.

Putto: A small boy. *Putti* in art are Cupid-like figures used for decoration. They frequently adorn paintings, sculpture, carved furniture, porcelain and silver, and occur in profusion in baroque decoration.

Queen's Ware: The trade name for the cream ware made by Wedgwood.

Reeding: A decoration made up of a series of convex parallel mouldings in relief.

Refectory Table: A large long rectangular table, often of oak, used for dining large parties. They were originally used by monks in monastic establishments.

Rent Table: A round or octagonal table – also called a capstan or drum table because of its shape – around which fit a series of wedge-shaped drawers. The top is supported on a central column or stand and has a round lidded hole in the centre into which the money was heaped. Rent tables usually stood in the hall of a country home and rent books and monies of each tenant were kept in one of the lockable drawers.

Reserve: A price placed by the vendor upon an object to be offered at auction, below which he is not prepared to sell.

Resist: A lustre decoration in which the ground colour shows through as the pattern.

Repoussé: Embossed work on metals such as silver or copper.

Reproduction: A fair copy of an original.

Ribboned: A term used to describe decoration in the form of trailing ribbons and bows.

Right: Genuine.

Ring: A group of people, usually dealers, who elect one bidder in advance of a sale to avoid the price being raised as a result of competition between them. See also *Knockout.*

Rococo: A style of decoration made up of flowing

symmetrical curves, delicately balanced so as not to disturb the flow or line of the object.

Roundel: A circular decorative panel or medallion.

Rummer: A large short-stemmed glass which came into fashion in the late eighteenth century. It derives its name from the traditional Rhenish wine glass. Many people wrongly associate the name with the drinking of rum toddy.

Salt Glaze: The frosty glaze achieved on early pottery and porcelain by throwing salt into the kiln during the firing.

Salver: A tray, sometimes standing on feet, for handing round drinks, etc.

Sampler: An embroidered panel; most frequently a child's needlework exercise.

Sconce: The part of a candlestick on which, or into which, the candle is placed. The word is sometimes used to describe the complete candlestick fitment when attached to a wall.

Scrapper: The term applied to a gold or silver object which is either badly worn or of no re-sale value and which will be consigned to a box of similar metal to be sold for its scrap weight value.

Scroll Feet: Feet resembling rolled up scrolls of paper or vellum (see Fig 6i).

Seal-top: The name given to an early type of spoon in which the finial is shaped like a seal.

Serpentine: A term used to describe the front of a piece of furniture of which the two ends curve inwards and the centre curves outwards all in one flowing line.

Settle: A chest with lid which also has arms and a back so that it can be used both for storage and as a seat.

Shagreen: A skin covering often used for small boxes and wallets. It is usually green or black and is thought by many to be the skin of the shark. Although this is sometimes true, it is more often ordinary animal skin into

which seeds have been pressed and the whole then
coloured.

Ship's Decanter: A decanter with a very broad base and
sloping sides, often known as a Rodney. It was less
likely to tip over in rough seas than an ordinary decanter (see Fig 13i).

Skewer: A large, silver-plated, flat-bladed object with a
ring handle which was pushed through barons of beef
to secure them for carving. They are now popular for
use as paper knives.

Skillet: A metal pot with a cover and a long handle, a
forerunner of the modern saucepan. They often had
feet. Seventeenth-century silver skillets are greatly
prized.

Skirt: The pieces of wood around a chair below the
seat. The front skirt is normally referred to as the
apron.

Slip: A creamy mixture of clay and water trailed over the
surface of pottery as decoration.

Snuffers: A cone of metal used to extinguish a candle
flame without damaging the wick, or a pair of tongs
(rather like sugar tongs) with flat blades which trim-
med the wick. Later examples were rather like a pair
of scissors with a box on one blade. The blades cut off
the charred portion of the wick which was caught and
extinguished in the box.

Soapstone: A soft stone which is easily carved. Most
soapstone carvings come from the East.

Spandrels: Decoration which radiates from and is
confined to the corners of a square or rectangle – eg,
the relief ormolu ornaments mounted in the corners of
a clock face.

Spelter: A cheap alloy, mainly of zinc.

Splat: The panel of wood running down the centre of an
open chair at the back.

Squab: A stuffed cushion.

Standish: An inkstand on four small feet and with a curved edge.

Stirrup Cup: A drinking vessel without a base to stand on, used by members of a hunt when in the saddle. They may be of glass, silver, porcelain or pottery and often take the form of an animal's head, particularly, of course, the fox.

Straw-work: A form of delicate marquetry where the design is built up from straw which has previously been dyed different colours.

Stretcher: The horizontal pieces of wood used to brace the legs of chairs, tables, etc.

Stringing: A thin band of inlay usually no more than one-eighth of an inch wide used to decorate the edges of furniture. Brass strips were also used for the same purpose, particularly during the Regency period.

Style: A term used in auction sale catalogues to convey their belief that the article is not of the period although the design and general appearance might lead one to believe it to be genuine – eg, a *Sheraton-style* china cabinet could have been made by a Victorian or Edwardian cabinet-maker.

Swagged: Festooned with flowers, fruit, leaves or draping.

Syllabub Glass: A small glass used for serving syllabub, a dish made with cream, wine and sugar.

Taking bids off the ceiling: When an auctioneer takes an imaginary bid in an attempt to raise the genuine bids. Also referred to as 'off the wall'.

Tallboy: An eighteenth-century piece of furniture which was made up of two chests-of-drawers, one above the other, the whole standing on bracket feet.

Tantalus: An open stand in which decanters were kept. It had a bar fitted with a lock which prevented anyone from removing the decanters and stealing the liquor, and was called a tantalus because it was tantalizing to see the liquor without being able to imbibe.

Taper Stick: A miniature candlestick for holding tapers.

Taper Jack: A box or stand which contained a rolled-up taper which could be pulled out as required. Sometimes called a waxjack.

Tazza: A saucer-shaped bowl or cup, usually mounted on a foot. Originally an early wine cup with a round shallow bowl.

Teapoy: A pedestal table with a lifting top which forms a large tea caddy containing compartments for tea and a mixing bowl.

Terracotta: A hard earthenware fired once. It is usually a brownish-red colour.

Toddy Lifter: A hollow tube with a bulbous end and a hole at each end used (rather like a pipette in a laboratory) to lift hot toddy from bowl to glass. The bulbous end was immersed in the toddy, and a finger was then placed over the hole at the top to prevent air from entering. The finger was removed to release the toddy.

Torchère: A tall column surmounted with a small round platform on which a candlestick could be placed to illuminate part of a room. They were generally made in pairs.

Totter: A 'rag and bone' man. Totters now deal mainly in scrap metal but usually keep an eye open for antiques and generally appreciate their value.

Trade Plate: The label fixed by a cabinet-maker on a piece of furniture he has made. Trade plates are often found beneath the frame.

Treen: A generic name for all small domestic articles made of wood.

Trivet: A stand, usually of iron or brass, which was kept in the hearth for hot saucepans and kettles.

Tunbridge Ware: Decorated woodwork which was made

in Tunbridge Wells from about 1680 until the 1890s.
The early work was marquetry but the best known is
the wood mosaic made in the nineteenth century. The
method was to build up a bundle of multi-coloured
strips of wood to create a picture at the end, rather like
the lettering in a stick of rock. The bundle was then secured and thin sections were sliced off and stuck to the
object to be decorated. This bundle gave many ident-
ical mosaics as the result of a single design operation.

Tyg: An early drinking vessel with three or more
handles.

Vellum: Cured skin used for early manuscripts.

Vinaigrette: A small box, often resembling a snuff box,
usually in precious metal or enamel but always gilded
on the inside. Inside the main lid was a secondary lid
pierced to allow perfume to rise from a sponge soaked
in scented vinegar which was held inside.

Vitrine: A display cabinet with glazed door and sides.

Volute: In the form of a scroll.

Waiter: A small silver salver.

Waxjack: See *Taper Jack*.

Weeder: A dealer who puts aside the best goods for his
own use.

Wine Cooler: A vessel, often of silver or plate, but sometimes of wood lined with lead. Bottles were placed in
the cooler and ice was packed around them.

Work Table: A small table, often supported by a single
pillar. The top formed the lid of a shallow box for
holding needles, cotton, etc, and beneath the box hung
a bag of material which would slide out. This was for
keeping the wools and silks used for embroidery.

Wrong: An adjective used to describe an antique or any
part of an antique which is not genuine.

INDEX

THE MOST SOUGHT AFTER SERIES IN THE '70's

These superb David & Charles titles are now available in PAN, for connoisseurs, enthusiasts, tourists and everyone looking for a deeper appreciation of Britain than can be found in routine guide books.

BRITISH STEAM SINCE 1900   W. A. Tuplin   45p
An engrossing review of British locomotive development – 'Intensely readable' – *Country Life*. Illustrated.

LNER STEAM   O. S. Nock   50p
A masterly account with superb photographs showing every aspect of steam locomotive design and operation on the LNER.

THE SAILOR'S WORLD   T. A. Hampton   35p
A guide to ships, harbours and customs of the sea. 'Will be of immense value' – *Port of London Authority*. Illustrated.

OLD DEVON   W. G. Hoskins   45p
'As perfect an account of the social, agricultural and industrial grassroots as one could hope to find' – *The Field*. Illustrated.

INTRODUCTION TO INN SIGNS
Eric R. Delderfield   35p
This beautifully illustrated and fascinating guide will delight everyone who loves the British pub. Illustrated.

THE CANAL AGE   Charles Hadfield   50p
A delightful look at the waterways of Britain, Europe and North America from 1760 to 1850. Illustrated.

RAILWAY ADVENTURE   L. T. C. Rolt   35p
The remarkable story of the Talyllyn Railway from inception to the days when a band of local enthusiasts took over its running. Illustrated.